SEEDTIME

Liberating the Oppressed

Anthony KaDarrell Thigpen

David William Austin, Co-Author

"My house shall be called a house of prayer,
but you have made it a den of thieves" (Luke 19:46).

IV

"Am I therefore become your enemy
because I tell you the truth" (Galatians 4:16).

1. Library of Congress Cataloging-in-Publication Data
2. All scriptures referenced throughout this book have been quoted from the King James Version Bible.
3. All biographical accounts referenced throughout this book are that of the author, Anthony KaDarrell Thigpen.

Copyright Ready Manuscripts
Eagle-Copy-Services
Minneapolis, Minnesota

ISBN: 978-0-9777697-4-2
1.   Christians - Religious Life.
Printed in the United States of America

Published by
LITERACY-IN-MOTION
"Publishing Perfection"

PO Box 11892
Merrillville, IN 46411-1892
posttribune@hotmail.com

seedtime

anthony kadarrell thigpen

david william austin
co-author

Special thanks to everyone who contributed
thoughts, suggestions, and helped during
the editorial process of this project.

Dedication
Wanting More

Wanting More

I'm confident that I'm losing my first-mind
I've convinced myself I'd be better off blind
This is one instance
When resistance
Makes me feel like I'm dying
So, I keep trying and crying
I'm blinking
And winking
My eyes
Hoping that my Savior will realize
That I'm trying not to compromise
I'm surprised
You haven't read between the lines
I know my Lord can read my mind
But sometimes
I wonder if it's possible for a mortal like me to have any-
thing in common
Perhaps it is just my comments
Maybe I'm thirsty to know your intents
Or could our acquaintance simply be a coincidence
No. This is much too intense
For instance
Why do I possess such a spiritual interest?
And did I mention
Master, you have my undivided attention
I'm hoping for more of your aggression
I'm trying to passively learn a powerful lesson

But I feel some sort of source pulling me away
So, I lift my hands higher and continue giving you praise
You are no risk to me
Your words they set me free
You've walked on tiptoes into small corners of my mind
This relationship is worth all of my time
And I'm amazed at how you consistently call me friend
Again and again
I keep rededicating my heart
Even from the start
I felt you changing me
You gave your name to me
Jesus, you sacrificed
Your earthly life
To even the score
Now, everything about you keeps me wanting more.

Table of Contents

XIV

About the Author
Anthony KaDarrell Thigpen

Pilgrimage to Justice

During my childhood, we never had much, but my mother's acts of kindness made us feel quite wealthy. Helping others became a part of my identity at an early age. As a Gulf War veteran, I understand the sacrifices required to liberate the oppressed—even amongst radical religious groups. As a young adult, I failed to study the Bible for myself. As a result, televangelist distracted me. Before I knew it, I was guilty of focusing on riches. I stumbled into debt with a high-interest Beneficial loan. I gave the large sum of money to my church, hoping to hit the heavenly jackpot. Well, it sounded good at the time. Financial prosperity messages perilously oppress people. When these *Name it and Claim it* messages started sweeping the nation, I gambled away my good credit. It took years before I climbed out my pitfall of deception. Now that I chase what matters, I understand. Hard-earned wages is how people with integrity purchase possessions. More importantly, family, friends, and fellowship mean more than money. As a journalist, while writing for the Indiana Post-Tribune, life took on new meaning. Unfortunately, I've exposed ousted pastors, church disputes, and infidelity inside the world of religion. I prefer feature stories, but we report the news, and church news is no exception. My editors, Charmella Greer and the late Richard Grey sent me on several story assignments to one specific church. They warned me. Local suspicions spiraled throughout the community, falsely labeling the Want-To-Be Mega-Church as a cult. The 1,200 member church owned a private school. About 16-months later, I married the principal, Clara (Blackmon). I abandoned my own church and joined forces. I was immediately placed in a key leadership role. Soon after, I chose a volunteer editorial position at the church, over revenue and popularity from the newspaper. I published the pastors' books, marketing materials, and other church literature. Suddenly, the spirit of my church began to change. Like so many other churches that build large facilities, the financial strain of high mortgages dictate the content of the sermons. Even worse, my wife and I were summoned to a private meeting with the senior pastors. We thought the unexpected meeting was to reward our selfless sacrifices. We were wrong. They falsely accused us of failing to tithe. Our contribution records were inaccurate, and we felt forced to prove otherwise. We made lump sum contributions, as opposed to the mandatory bi-weekly payments. I was shocked—I'm still shocked. The next day, an associate pastor called. I was genuinely honored by the request to become a deacon. However, I'm not a deacon. I declined the ordination. Perhaps my acceptance would have served as their apology. Instead, I felt charged to change the way churchgoers view money. For six months, church services were unpleasant. Negative remarks echoed across the bully pulpit as public persecution. The love of money redefined our church. I made peace with the pastors. However, it is clear that something unhealthy transpired in our relationship. After 7-years of successfulness, my wife resigned as principal. Maybe my more-experienced editors saw something I could not. As a love-struck reporter, I compromised. Nonetheless, prior to the makeover, our church was a more attractive place to worship. Your outlook on money can make you forget what matters most. Behind the closed doors of prosperity churches, the only acceptable influence comes across the pulpit. No questions allowed—not even during Bible study. Suggestions are considered rebellion and gossip. These are the complicated components that make this secretive subject so difficult to discuss. Despite their outlook on money, the church continues to give to the community. Perhaps the pastors' good works are a reflection of their kind hearts. On the other hand, many churches invest in marketing ploys to gain membership and make more money. Nonetheless, I refuse to ignore organized religion. Churches possess the ability to serve a significant role in communities throughout America. However, to do so, the focus must remain on spiritual principles, not money. More than 15-years-ago, my friend Ernest Googe was misdiagnosed with a common cold. His condition was far more complicated. He actually needed a heart transplant. I sold all of my possessions, quit my job, moved to Texas, and ministered love and life by his hospital bedside. Money has absolutely nothing to do with ministry. Countless Christians are trapped in pitfalls of prosperity which is the most complicated form of religious oppression. It teaches people of faith to focus on physical results. Financial challenges during childhood taught me that hope and happiness is not predicated on physical possessions. Lack taught me lessons that all the money in the world cannot erase. Dr. Martin Luther King Jr., Malcolm X, and Marcus Garvey understood that money is not the mark of influence. Like Jesus, every great leader possesses a passion to liberate the oppressed.

About The Co-Author
David Austin

Liberating the Oppressed

Oppression is defined as the use of power to subjugate, marginalize or silence. It dominates individuals and groups of people. It is often used to empower the oppressor. The root word of oppression is press. To press is an action-verb which describes the process of reducing the size of an object. This new-aged prosperity theology has two opposing logics. It forces people to give money in order to get more in return. Furthermore, it mentally stresses others who do not have anything to give in the first place. Oppression paralyzes people who get caught between this illogical premise. Growing up in a starch, legalistic, Pentecostal church is challenging, to say the least. I felt tormented by inferiority and plagued with self-doubt. The Mosaic Law in conjunction with church rules imposed stiff stipulations. It placed a serious strain on my psyche. Nobody preached grace in our Pentecostal circle. She was like an undisclosed mistress. Acknowledging her would contradict most everything our church believed. As a result, grace remained a secret. My childhood church systematically oppressed parishioners. Throughout this book, names are not mentioned, but there are many churches just like it. Religious oppression is a combination of institutional, social, and economic pressure. Our church operated like a modern-day monarchy. The pastor ruled with complete authority. Incidentally, my father served as an assistant pastor under the senior pastor. Without question, there was no room for questions. Those who did so were publicly labeled as heretics. Unfortunately, control tactics permeate across the pulpit into the pews. God gives all men the freedom of choice. This same freedom of choice is extended to people who refuse relationship with him—God is an unconditional advocate for choice. My religious family rejected the notion of free-will. We were advocates of discipline and control. Subservience is the theme of legalism, not love. Subsequently, our loveless home focused on obedience. Oppression strips people of personal identity. As a result, the cult-like church destroyed the concept of a healthy and loving childhood. It damaged our lives. My parents divorced. Even worse, the controlling church still managed to oppress my father. Perhaps people who control others don't realize the damage they cause. Nonetheless, oppression sabotages families. I was caught in the middle of a broken marriage and two completely different perspectives about religion. The affects of oppression during my childhood caused identity loss and insecurity. Years later, as an adult, I searched beyond the confusion and frustration hoping to discover a more meaningful life. I escaped judgmental churches, only to stumble into others like it. Ignorance kept me bound by day—I wrestled with the fear of eternal damnation by night. My thoughts were cluttered and I suffered a severe case of mixed emotions. With no uncertainty, my mind was blinded by the bondage imposed by religious oppression. It gets even worse. Despite the fact that I loved the Lord, religious oppression made me feel forced to think negative thoughts. For example, as an innocent little boy, I remember preachers shouting and pointing, with congregants applauding and screaming "Amen." The crafty persuasiveness of these legalistic sermons used threat tactics to gain expected results. Legalistic sermons about hell, fire, and brimstone defined my childhood depiction of God. Based on their standards, a mischievous child couldn't possibly please God. Therefore, I deemed myself worthless. After years of misguided thinking, I continued my personal quest for God. I prematurely searched in churches. It took even more years before I decided to diligently study the Bible for myself. Meanwhile, I isolated myself from people who loved me. I didn't know anything about love. As a result, I rejected it. On the other hand, I knew a lot about religious oppression. It seems as though some magnetic attraction allured me back to controlling churches. There I sat again, as if I were under some sort of hypnosis, allowing religious leaders to control my destiny. I could not find contentment, because I refused to look for it in Christ alone. So, my search began again. This has been no easy journey. However, God rewards those who diligently seek him. I'm not sure if I discovered *Truth*, or if it rescued me. Nonetheless, I'm free. Eventually, I started studying the Bible without motive or pretense. Suddenly, I began to see life through a different lens. My eyes are open. The frustration faded, confusion collapsed, and I am no longer barricaded by religious bondage. However, I feel a strong sense of obligation to liberate others. Recently, I joined forces with a friend, author Anthony KaDarrell Thigpen. After about eight months of research and writing, he asked me to help with *Seedtime*. This book is far more liberating than I ever imagined. Although we attended the same church, previous conversations never included dialogue about financial prosperity or religious oppression. Despite our surroundings, we remained focused.

God's plan is to combat religious oppression and spread good news to the poor. This book is an attack on Satan's strategy against the Saints. We avoided slandering the names of oppressive culprits, because we aim to demonstrate God's love to everyone. *Seedtime* uses the means of biblical education to relieve the oppressed. People of faith must stand up against injustices. We must annihilate our personal feelings and biases in order to see what God sees. If while reading this book, you recognize that you've been guilty, repent and move on. Men who are deceived will undoubtedly deceive others. Hence, the vicious cycle continues. If the blind leads the blind then both will fall into a ditch. I stopped lying to myself, and I ignore the lies of others. Even when lies echo across pulpits, I rely on the Bible for accuracy, accept the truth, and then share it with others. This is the reason God gives Christians the gift of the Holy Spirit; to heal the broken-hearted; to preach good news to the poor; to liberate the oppressed; and to set the captives free. Remember, the truth will make you free (see John 8:32). Jesus does not merely expect us to know the truth, he commissions us to help people who are bound by injustices.

Introduction

Horrified by Oppression
& Passionate About Justice

SEEDTIME

Seedtime is nearly 300-pages of extensive biblical research. This book illustrates the relevance of God's word today. God does not change. Despite popular opinion, the complete message of the Bible warns against chasing high hopes of selfish gain. J.P. Morgan Chase recently implemented a marketing campaign that psychologically encourages people to focus on wealth—rightfully so. The financial institution specializes in retail, commercial, and investment banking. In 2008, the campaign slogan changed from *Your Choice Your Chase* to *Chase What Matters*. To their own shame, prosperity churches are chasing the same corruptible wealth as secular society. This new-aged prosperity movement is centered on earthly affections. By its nature, preaching financial prosperity opposes the true message of the gospel. God is not opposed to wealth. However, money has absolutely nothing to do with God's message of love. Therefore, churches must be careful not to magnify money over the Master, especially in the pulpit. The only way to liberate the oppressed is to educate true believers about God's word. Leaders teach financial prosperity in economically challenged communities for two reasons. Some do so to change the poverty stricken mindset of poor people—they have good intentions. Others misuse scriptures to persuade people, and then manipulate members out of money. These people pervert the pulpit with luxurious lifestyles of filthy lucre. Both kinds of prosperity preachers are dead wrong. Although some leaders mean well, any theology focused on physical possessions result in carnal expectations. It blinds the minds of people with secular ambitions, physical desires, lustful pleasures,

worldly affection, and outright greediness (see II Corinthians 3:14). Ultimately, the financial prosperity theology
forces believers to set their sights on perishable possessions.
Instead, we should seek spiritual promises—the Kingdom
of God and his righteousness. The moral fiber within the
Christian community is suffocated when Christians chase
money. *"For the love of money is the root of all evil: which while some
coveted after, they have erred from the faith, and pierced themselves
through with many sorrows"* (I Timothy 6:10). *Seedtime* will teach
you how to chase what matters to God. The modern-day
Christian community is suffering from socioeconomic and
religious oppression. These injustices include money manipulation, religious deception, bully pulpits and mind-
control tactics, to say the least. Ultimately, this new-aged
financial prosperity gospel causes oppression. Unfortunately,
the advocates of this message think money is God's plan of
liberation. Therefore, they continue to compel listeners.
They distort the meaning of the Bible by cherry-picking
scriptures and teaching text out of context. They fail to realize that their messages do more damage than good. During
my first mission trip, natives instructed us not to give money
to indigenous Guatemalan women and children. Despite the
fact that financial contributions would have eliminated
much of their suffering, other elements were at work. Our
good intentions would have certainly produced temporary
results, but long term woes, as well. Indigenous groups living in poverty, barely surviving in half-built homes, are fortunate if they earn $4 per day. When people give to others,
they must consider the fundamental principles of sociology.

Otherwise, it is easy to misconstrue charity with financial contributions—they are not the same. A $100 contribution to an innocent barefoot child, degrades the systemic integrity of an indigenous culture. Considering immaturity and limited education, poor children aspire to live life like wealthy mission workers. In reality, their contributions send mixed signals about money. Most mission workers are not wealthy at all. However, when men and women give $100 bills to children who do nothing to earn it, they devalue work ethics. In America, this same concept applies to drug dealers, prostitutes, and those who flock after the prosperity gospel. It teaches people that they can get something for little to nothing. In these remote Guatemalan villages, it weakens the morale of men who work more than 200 hours to earn $100. Guilt-driven mission workers can ruin socioeconomic climates. As a result, it demeans the value of Guatemalan men. These same men, are the backbone of their indigenous communities. After the $100 is spent, and mission workers return home, Guatemalans must rely on their own indigenous system to survive. If money alone could solve an economic crisis, mission workers could merely send money and save travel expenses. Economically oppressed people need education, not financial hand-outs. The same principles apply to socioeconomic and religious oppression in the United States. The 2008 economic bailout plan failed to bolster economic support for America's banking industry. Afterward, President George W. Bush officially announced that the USA is suffering from an economic recession. President Barack Obama inherited America's economic crisis in

2009. With the support of the democratic party, he implemented a nearly $800 billion stimulus plan. A socialist perspective of spreading wealth does not solve economic crisis. Giving money to greedy corporate criminals will never solve the inherent problem of greed. Money incriminates people who have pledged allegiance to prosperity. Whereas American International Group (AIG) received more than $150 Billion in bailout money in 2008. Afterward, top executive walked away with bonuses in excess of a $1 million. The major insurance corporation withstood public reprimand when they requested additional revenue from taxpayers. Democratic Congressman Paul Hodes said, AIG will forever stand for "Arrogance, incompetence and greed." A redistribution of wealth is not the solution to a misappropriation of resources. For this reason, financial prosperity can never become the primary focus of any group who aims to liberate the oppressed. According to the Bible, even the words of Jesus, Christians are supposed to liberate the oppressed (see Isaiah 58:6, Luke 4:18). Instead, we do more harm than good with messages of financial prosperity. This book is not about slandering those who meander the truth. The first step toward liberation is education. This book utilizes the Bible, life stories of Anthony KaDarrell Thigpen, historical facts, and current events to educate readers. Oppression is horrifying. This is why Christians must become passionate about justice. The twelve chapters included in this book are written in Reader-Focused-Writing. To help readers best understand the Bible, we've used a textbook format. The alliteration arrangements makes reading easy and memora-

ble. The first four foundational chapters provide an introduction to the mechanics of Christian theology. These 4-
chapters explain the Bible from a contextual perspective.
Chapter 5 helps readers transition from the theological introduction to the general theme of *Seedtime*—combating the
theology of prosperity. Chapters 6-7 describe the historical
details of the ancient tithe and modern-day money miscon-
ceptions. Chapter 8 illuminates the difference between
physical possessions and spiritual promises. Chapter 9 is a
biblical overview that defines the spiritual judgment needed
to access the kingdom of God. Chapter 10 is designed to
teach religious leaders the critical importance of accountability. Chapter 11 unveils God's road to redemption. Finally,
chapter 12 represents the twelfth gate to God's kingdom—
the power of government intervention. The chapters are
arranged to enable readers to visualize the reality that the
prosperity theology is not a route to the kingdom of God.
The sub-titles, sentence structures, and appendixes will help
people who are in search of something more valuable than
money. As a result of the oppression slavery imposed, Mississippi had more millionaires per capita than any other state
in the Union. Slavery is one the worse forms of oppression
in history. The Civil War of 1862 caused many to die in pursuit to liberate the oppressed. On the other hand, men who
ruthlessly chase riches die with their dreams. Individuals
who dedicate their lives liberating the oppressed, leave lega-
cies that others glean from for generations. *Seedtime* will arm
you with the weapon needed to fight religious oppression.

Chapter **1**

The Right Resource for Revelation

SEEDTIME

The Kiss that Changed my Life

As Christians, it's easy to slip into a religious rut. Most of us have experienced the uncomfortable sensation of feeling spiritually stuck. Recently, my church transformed from being mission oriented to prosperity centered. The silhouette of Sunday morning sermons malformed from the theme of Christ to currency. The city of Babylon is referenced as the great whore in the Book of Revelation (see Revelation 17:1-5). A whore has one distinct characteristic. Whores trade intimacy for money. God wants us to maintain a meaningful relationship with him. Intimacy is meaningless to whores who sale themselves for money. Babylon represents people who exchange spiritual promises for physical pleasures. People should not go to church week after week meaninglessly volunteering in ministries. It is shameful to sashay through the Bible without gaining an understanding (see II Timothy 2:15, Proverbs 4:7). I've found myself trapped in this deep-dark pit even as a successful journalist and a committed Christian. Recently, life took on new meaning. Instead of commitment, I decided to surrender. I no longer want to be in charge, in command or even in control. I simply want to lift my hands, kneel in submission, and surrender to God's will. Commitments are choices we make based on circumstances. When people surrender, their circumstances no longer matter. God is not merely looking for committed Christians, he's looking for believers who are willing to do his will despite difficult challenges. Believers who surrender are at the mercy of the Master, despite the opinions of men. According to Hebrew translations, worship means to kiss. In other words, to become intimately connected to the lover of the soul. Either we worship or kiss God, or we give in to the seduction of Babylon the great whore. Remember, never kiss a whore. I served in many churches as a committed Christian. It wasn't until recently that I truly surrendered. When you surrender to God, he will consume your life. Volunteerism in churches does not define a surrendered Christian. Nothing matters more than relationship with God, especially to those who have been kissed by his kindness. Otherwise, religion is nothing more than a boring, mundane, and purposeless way of life. Not so—the reason you feel like something is missing is because something is missing. My family lives a quite comfortable life. My wife is an educator, I'm the surrogate father of a son who attends the University of Southern Indiana, and our daughter is a healthy and energetic 3-year-old. We have the family, finances and lifestyle that others passionately dream about, but none of these things fulfill us–only God. It is so easy to slip and slide into worldly ambitions. Don't allow desires of financial prosperity, companionship or glamorous lifestyles to redirect your spiritual destiny. Allow that first kiss to take complete control of your heart and mind. This book will teach you how to surrender to God. Afterward, he will take you from the rut of religion to the cleft of the rock.

Seeking the Secret Place

King David desperately wanted to dwell in God's secret place. In fact, he referred to it as his only spiritual desire (see Psalms 27:4). Most Christians falsely assume that the house of the Lord is the visible church. Not so. *"God that made the world and all things therein, seeing that he is Lord of heaven and earth, dwells not in temples made with hands"* (Acts 17:24). The secret place is not physical, but it does not have to be foreign to believers. Unfortunately, many Christians today are focused on physical possessions rather than spiritual promises. Stop begging for hand-outs and start seeking a face-to-face encounter with God. When Moses asked God to show him his glory, God responded, *"Thou cannot see my face: For there shall no man see me, and live"* (Exodus 33:20). For this reason, God instructed Moses to stand on a rock. He promised to hide him in the cleft of the rock and allow him to see his backside. Stop living hand-to-mouth and seek what matters. When we seek that secret place where God reveals his glory, nothing matters but personal relationship, spiritual redemption, and the willingness to suffer (see Exodus 35:5). The house of the Lord is where his glory is hidden. In order to dwell in the secret place, you must position yourself upon the rock.

Reasons Readers Don't Understand the Bible

The Bible is one the most well-read literary compositions in the world. Scholars and laymen alike, use it as a roadmap to understand historical, cultural, figurative, archeological and religious perspectives. Despite one's passion to read, people without revelation are without relationship with God. Man cannot live by bread alone (see Matthew 4:4). Comprehension of the Bible can be acquired through education, translation, interpretation and information. However, the Bible enables true believers to experience revelation. Unfortunately, casual readers, archeologist and scholars forfeit what matters most. Despite their discoveries, they fail to believe the spiritual validity of the Bible. The Bible was in fact written, translated and composed by ordinary men. However, it was inspired by God, who is extraordinary. He carefully orchestrated the Holy Bible with similar strategic efforts used in human creation. Even some Christians feed into skepticisms about the authors and attempt to discredit God's word. God uses ordinary people, but the Bible is certainly no ordinary book. The Holy Bible is sacred and divine. It nourishes the soul and spirit. People who try to process spiritual things with their natural faculties, always lack understanding about the written word. They miss what God desires to reveal. In many cases, the Bible does not possess smooth literary transitions. Revelation from God is what connects all 66-books. It is not intended for enemies or doubters of God to understand his secrets and mysteries. This is why Jesus only spoke in parables. *"And he said, Unto you it is given to know the mysteries of the kingdom of God: but to others in parables; that seeing they might not see, and hearing they might not understand"* (Luke 8:10). *Seedtime* is God's revelation about the financial prosperity movement. It illuminates the battle between the idol god of this physical world and God who is a Spirit. It highlights the contrast between greed and selflessness. It is also a guide to help curious, confident and confused people navigate through the Bible. *Seedtime* transforms an extraordinary book into the rock of our salvation. Never expect to understand spiritual things using natural resources.

Understanding the Rock that Matters

People are inclined to reject anything they do not understand. For this reason, civil rights leader Dr. Martin Luther King Jr. was martyred April 4, 1968. United States President John F. Kennedy was assassinated November 22, 1963. Even worse, in 33 A.D., a Roman governor, Pontius Pilate, in cooperation with Jewish leaders, crucified Jesus Christ. People who do not understand the Bible take the same approach to religion. They neglect what matters most. Do not ignore the parts of the Bible you do not understand. God's word is the rock upon which our foundation is built. God is referred to as the rock of our salvation (see Psalms 89:26, 95:1). Therefore, it is important to understand the significance of the word rock. Otherwise, the cliché, "Rock of my salvation," is nothing more than swelling words and a sweet phrase that sounds good. Dr. Martin Luther King Jr., John F. Kennedy, and Jesus Christ were all murdered because they spoke truthful words that conflicted with mainstream society. Understanding truth is critically important. If you fail to completely wrap your mind around a spiritual idea, you'll lose grip of meaningful thoughts.

The Biblical Definition of the Rock

Most people understand the basic definition of a rock. It is hard solid of natural origin made of minerals. However, various rocks differ from these three characteristics. They are not always hard. Some rocks can be scratched with your fingernail, such as shale, soapstone and gypsum. Others may be soft in the ground, but they harden once they spend time in the air, and vice versa. Some rocks are not completely solid. They include water in their pore spaces. Many geodes, or hollow objects, found in limestone country, hold water inside them like coconuts. Rocks are not even necessarily all natural. There are other complex components to rocks that geologists study, such as crystals with minerals and obsidian without minerals. This paragraph clearly demonstrates that there are different kinds of rocks. The rock of our salvation is spiritual. *"For they drank of that spiritual Rock that followed them: and that Rock was Christ"* (I Corinthians 10:4). Jesus Christ is the rock of ages.

Understanding the Spiritual Rock of Revelation

The spiritual rock is revelation. Jesus describes revelation as our power and protection. *"For flesh and blood has not revealed it unto thee, but my Father which is in heaven. ...And upon this rock I will build my church; and the gates of hell shall not prevail against it"* (Matthew 16:17-18). Water is figuratively used through-out scripture to describe the word of God (see Ephesians 5:26). Therefore, without the rock of revelation, people thirst. As a result, Israelites drank water from the rock (see Exodus 17:6). As believers, the rock is our foundation; therefore, we stand on the rock (see Exodus 33:21-22). Our lives are supposed to be centered on revelation. Hence, the Bible instructs us to speak to the rock (see Number 20:8, 11). People who live by faith dwell in the rock (see Numbers

24:21). God causes those who joyfully exalt him to extract revelation and anointing from the rock (see Deuteronomy 32:13 and 32:15). Be mindful of the rock (see Deuteronomy 32:18). Never allow false teachers to bind you with words and take you away from the rock (see Judges 15:13). Listen to the rock (see II Samuel 23:3). David conquered a giant enemy named Goliath with a smooth stone; our weapon is the rock (see I Samuel 17:1-58). Moreover, we ought to hide in the rock (see Jeremiah 13:4). *"Therefore whosoever hear these sayings of mine, and does them, I will liken him unto a wise man, which built his house upon a rock"* (Matthew 7:24). Others will be offended by this book. *"For their rock is not as our Rock"* (Deuteronomy 32:31). The stone that the builders rejected has become the chief corner stone (see Luke 20:17). Prosperity preachers who are bound by multi-million dollar mortgages often reject the rock. *"And a stone of stumbling, and a rock of offense, even to them which stumble at the word, being disobedient: whereunto also they were appointed"* (I Peter 2:8). When believers focus on physical ideas and possessions, they forfeit the spiritual rock of revelation. This book will give sight to people who are spiritually blind, but warning and judgment to churchgoers who neglect *Truth*.

Satan Stirs Confusion but God Confounds

Some people neglect *Truth*, claiming that the language used in the Bible is confusing. Others diligently seek even when they are confounded. Confusion is defined as unclear, jumbled or mixed together. Confound is to cause shame, defeat or overthrow. These two words are related as synonyms, but they are unrelated as it relates to scriptural use. The words confusion and confound are used completely different throughout the Bible. This is not just a case of mere semantics. Satan is the author of confusion. God is the author and finisher of our faith. Satan uses confusion to cause conflict, strife, contention and envy. God confounds in effort to redirect those he loves. The word confusion is used 25 times in the KJV Bible and the word confound is used 51 times. God never confuses. Satan never confounds. People who are confounded experience the same initial emotion as those who are confused. However, there is a distinct difference. Wickedness is the fruit of confusion. People who are confounded are forcefully redirected. Most people pretend as though they are confused when God speaks, because spiritual choices are sometimes difficult to make. Where there is confusion you will witness every evil work. God confounds in effort to turn his people away from the works of the enemy.

The Confounded Church

God confounded the children of Zerubbabel. They attempted to build the Tower of Babel. They aspired to acquire spiritual things by physical means. Perhaps such an effort would be possible, if God were to allow it. Instead, he forbids it. He stops it. He confounds Christians who attempt to do it. *"Therefore is the name of it called Babel; because the Lord did there confound the language of all the earth: and from thence did the Lord scatter them abroad upon the face of all the earth"* (Genesis 11:9). It is important to notice that the people of Babel substituted brick for stone (see Genesis 11:3). There is no substitution for revelation. You can give all of your money and possessions to prosperity preachers, but that will not quantify blessings from God. When you desire to build yourself up in God always use the right resources. Remember, *"For their rock is not as our Rock, even our enemies themselves being judges"* (Deuteronomy 32:31). Store-fronts and mega-churches must build healthy congregations with the same resources. Revelation from God is our most relevant resource. For this reason, God is the architect of our destiny. In order to see what God sees, one must be willing to endure a painful journey. Otherwise, God confounds the works of vanity, destroys the monuments of men, and redirects selfish-ambition. Unlike mankind, God is not a show-off. Everything he does is by way of purpose and design. His relationship with us is not based on might or power, but by his spirit (see Zechariah 4:6). Signs and wonders do indeed follow believers (see Mark 16:17). However, we should never set our sights on physical results. In other words, there are consequences for people who focus on physical facts instead of spiritual promises (see Genesis 19:26, Luke 9:62, Philippians 3:14). Many Christians seek after signs, wonders, large crowds and financial wealth. As such, they fail to chase what matters to the creator. God speaks with a still small voice (see I Kings 19:12). *"For who hath despised the day of small things"* (Zechariah 4:10). God promised to make the mountain of Zerubbabel a level plain and to instruct the people to rebuild it (see Zechariah 4:7-9). He wants you to build, but with the right resource. When God redirects, will you harden your heart like Pharaoh, the King of Egypt? God is confounding the modern-day church because many Christians have given in to prosperity messages. Many churchgoers, even leaders, are inundated with ambitions of prosperity. People are more interested in building wealth than laying a solid foundation. What is your salvation built on, physical possessions or spiritual promises? Don't make the same mistake as the people of Babel. The Bible states that they substituted brick for stone. Nothing can replace revelation from God. There rock is not our Rock.

General Information about Sedimentary Rocks

For ages, little pieces of the earth have been eroding—broken down and worn away by wind and water. These little bits of earth are washed downstream. Afterward, they settle at the bottom of rivers, lakes and oceans. There are layers of eroded earth deposits. These layers are pressed down over time, until the bottom slowly turns into rock. Hence, rock is produced by water, wind and pressure. This book will explain why water, wind and pressure represent God's word, the Holy Spirit and suffering. This is how we acquire the right resource, which is revelation.

General Information about Igneous Rocks

Igneous rocks are called fire rocks. They are formed under and above ground. Underground, they are formed when melted rock, called magma, is trapped in small pockets. As these pockets of magma slowly cool, the magma becomes igneous rocks. Remember, the manifestation of igneous rocks require heat. Igneous rocks are also formed when volcanoes erupt. Afterward, magma rises above the earth's surface. When magma appears above the earth, it is called lava. Igneous rocks are formed as the lava cools above ground. Heat purges. This book explains why revelation is needed in order to cleanse Christians from worldliness.

General Information about Metamorphic Rocks

Metamorphic rocks "morph" into another kind of rock. These rocks were once igneous or sedimentary rocks. "How do sedimentary and igneous rocks change," you might ask? When rocks are under tons of pressure heat builds up. Pressure combined with heat causes change. If you exam metamorphic rock samples, you'll discover flattened grains. This book will explain why rock represents a combination of purging, extreme suffering, revelation from God, and spiritual principles.

The Church Built on the Rock

Churches that are not built on revelation, do not glorify God. *"When Jesus came into the coasts of Caesarea Philippi, he asked his disciples, saying, Whom do men say that I the Son of man am? And they said, Some say that thou art John the Baptist: some, Elijah; and others, Jeremiah, or one of the prophets. He said unto them, But whom say ye that I am"* (Matthew 16:13-15)? Believers today, respond to questions about Jesus' identity the same as the disciples. Too many people base their faith on what others say. Instead, we need revelation from God. Even some disciples who spent personal time with him did not intimately know him. Peter, whose name means rock, received revelation from God. *"And Simon Peter answered and said, Thou art the Christ, the Son of the living God. And Jesus answered and said unto him, Blessed art thou, Simon Bar-jona: for flesh and blood hath not revealed it unto thee, but my Father which is in heaven. And I say also unto thee, That thou art Peter, and upon this rock I will build my church; and the gates of hell shall not prevail against it"* (Matthew 16:16-18). The only thing that can withstand the judgment of God is revelation from God. Your body is the temple of God. You are the Church. Without a personal relationship with God life is meaningless. Revelation is the key to understanding the Bible. *Seedtime* will teach you how to build on the rock.

SEEDTIME

Chapter **2**

The Seed of Faith

SEEDTIME

Madoff Made Off like Prosperity Preachers

For almost 20-years, financier Bernard Madoff swindled American investors out of $68.4 billion. March 12, 2009, he pleaded guilty to the most spectacular swindle Wall Street has ever seen. Preaching prosperity in American pulpits is the most deceptive form of evil in the church. Madoff's scandal transformed the well-respected Jewish business-man—former chairman of the NASDAQ exchange, into a symbol of Wall Street greed. Similarly, American churches are transforming into icons of swindlers who misrepresent God. Madoff's crime was exposed amid America's eco-nomic meltdown. His victims included individuals, trusts, pension funds and nonprofit organizations. Much like Mad-off made off with billions from innocent investors, prosper-ity preachers manipulate millions from churchgoers. Mad-off's fraudulent scheme wiped out people's life savings, ru-ined charities, and at least two suicides are accredited to his crime. White House spokesman Robert Gibbs said, "The president (Barack Obama) is glad that swift justice will hap-pen." Madoff is expected to receive 150 years in prison. In-vestor DeWitt Baker claims personal loses of more than $1 million with Madoff. He said, "I'd stone him to death." Oth-ers belted out, "He's evil" and "I think he should rot in hell." Madoff's money madness destroyed many lives for filthy lucre. Every promise he persuaded clients to believe was false. The promises of prosperity preachers are no dif-ferent from Madoff's madness. Upon Madoff's conviction, Burt Ross, an Englewood, N.J. lawyer said, "It's a little bit like seeing the devil." It is important for Christians to under-stand the concept of how the Bible depicts two kinds of seed. Madoff is behind bars, but the religious battle between Satan's corruptible seed and the incorruptible seed of Christ continues (see Revelation 12:7). Pulpit officials misuse cor-ruptible seed in sermons to sway churchgoers to sow money. Afterward, they expect to reap a harvest of prosper-ity in return from their investment.

God's Word vs. Satan's Seed

The Bible uses the metaphor of seed to illustrate the rich-ness of God's word in opposition to Satan's worldly wealth. This sub-section transitions through a series of scripture to enable readers to clearly understand the biblical concept of seed. First, it is critical that Christians comprehend the strong sense of hatred that God infused between the two seeds. *"I (God) will put enmity between thee (Satan) and the woman, and between thy seed and her seed; it shall bruise thy head, and thou shalt bruise his heel"* (Genesis 3:15). Any slave that was pur-chased by Israelites with money was not considered seed based on God's standard (see Genesis 17:12). Money is never supposed to be associated with the seed of God's peo-ple. In fact, God instructed the children of Israel not to sow mingled seed. *"Ye shall keep my statutes. Thou shalt not let thy cattle engender with a diverse kind: thou shalt not sow thy field with mingled seed: neither shall a garment mingled of linen and woolen come upon thee"* (Leviticus 19:19). In other words, either believers sow incorruptible or corruptible seed—God's people do not mingle the sacred concept of spiritual principles with Satan's seed of physical temptation. As Christians, we are joint heirs with Christ. *"Being born again, not of corruptible seed, but of incorruptible, by the word of God, which live and abide forever"* (I Peter 1:23). We must be mindful that whatever we sow we will reap. Therefore, people who sow money will reap corruption and people who sow God's word will reap incorruptible promises. Giving money to godly causes is a good way to demonstrate kindness. On the other hand, there is a life threatening difference between corruptible and incorruptible seed—this is not a matter of semantics—it is an issue of salvation. *"When any one hear the word of the kingdom, and understand it not, then cometh the wicked one, and catch away that which was sown in his heart. This is he which received seed by the way side. (22) He also that received seed among the thorns is he that hear the word; and the care of this world, and the deceitfulness of riches, choke the word, and he become unfruitful"* (Matthew 13:19, 22). The devil deceptively misuses worldly wealth to confuse and convince Christians to counterfeit God's seed. Therefore, money-driven preachers misuse the Bible to chase prosperity. *"But he that received seed into the good ground is he that hear the word, and understand it; which also bear fruit, and bring forth, some a hundredfold some sixty, some thirty"* (Matthew 13:23). Despite the fact that the Bible continuously defines God's word as spiritual seed, prosperity preachers pervert pulpits and teach people that seed also represents money. True Christians refuse to compromise. People who study the Bible are able to identify the difference between Holy Seed, which is Jesus Christ, as opposed to the counterfeits of the anti-Christ.

"(Jesus) said, unto you it is given to know the mysteries of the kingdom of God: but to others in parables; that seeing they might not see, and hearing they might not understand. Now the parable is this: The seed is the word of God" (Luke 8:11). Beware of religious leaders who refuse this reality and continue to combine Christ with currency (see II Timothy 3:5). The NT reveals that Jesus Christ is the seed referenced in this text. *"Remember that Jesus Christ of the seed of David was raised from the dead according to my gospel"* (II Timothy 2:8). According to the gospel of John, Jesus Christ is also the word made flesh (see John 1:14). According to the Apostle Paul, turn away from false teachers who pervert the truth.

Artificial Insemination of Satan's Seed

There are two coastal Phoenician cities referenced throughout the Bible named Sidon and Tyre. The spelling of Tyre is also denoted as Tyrus in various biblical writings. Jezebel, the daughter of the Phoenician king, brought idol worship to Israel's courts when she married King Ahab. For 22-years, 874-853 B.C., Ahab reigned as king. One of Tyre's most coveted exports was purple dye—they specialized in making artificial possessions appear as though they were sacred artifacts. God called the spirit of Satan the Prince of Tyre, according to the Prophet Ezekiel (see Ezekiel 28:1-4). Tyre manipulated resources to gain riches, relationships, and superficial redemption. King Ahab implemented the idolatrous influence of Tyre in Israel. Some modern-day Christians continue to misuse money to establish connections, gain influence and rebuild reputations. This evil spirit reigns in the hearts of men and women who set their affections on earthly possessions (see Ezekiel 28:12-19, Colossians 3:2). Like Satan, they start off with divine revelation until they become possessed with the passion of financial prosperity. *"By the multitude of thy merchandise they have filled the midst of thee with violence, and thou hast sinned"* (Ezekiel 28:16). Jezebel's name means where is the prince? The spirit of Jezebel seeks to destroy the king's kids by controlling them with idolatrous ideas about prosperity. This spirit forces people of faith to think that earthly possessions are God's spiritual blessings. Sixty-one-years after the reign of King Ahab, in 792 B.C., Uzziah took the throne of Judah at age 16. He reigned during the time of great material prosperity. He built cities, fortified the walls of Jerusalem with towers, and re-built a major coastal port among other things. Whereas God's people focused on physical prosperity as opposed to spirituality (see Isaiah 6:11-13). *"For the vineyard of the Lord of hosts is the house of Israel (God's chosen people), and the men of Judah (Praise) his pleasant plant: and he looked for judgment, but behold oppression; for righteousness, but behold a cry. (13) Therefore my people are gone into captivity, because they have no knowledge: and their honorable men are famished, and their multitude dried up with thirst. Therefore hell hath enlarged herself, and opened her mouth without measure: and their glory, and their multitude, and their pomp, and he that rejoices, shall descend into it"* (Isaiah 5:7, 13-14). When people made physical possessions their priority during the days of King Uzziah, it prevented Israelites from seeing life from a spiritual perspective. *"In the year that king Uzziah died I saw also the Lord sitting upon a throne, high and lifted up, and his train filled the temple"* (Isaiah 6:1). In 33 AD, Jesus informed NT Jews of his judgment concerning the generation that markets praise attempting to manipulate physical results (see Matthew 11:16-17). These are people that praise God with physical expectations. They understand the physical aspect of praise—playing instruments, dancing, singing and crying. However, instead of spiritually focusing on whom God is, they praise with expectation of physical results. *"But I say unto you, It shall be more tolerable for Tyre and Sidon at the day of judgment, than for you"* (Matthew 11:22). The name Tyre or Tyrus means *rock*, as in revelation. However, some preachers pollute God's word with aspirations of wealth. *"For their rock is not as our Rock"* (Deuteronomy 32:31). Modern-day churches are like the people of Tyre that trade revelation from God for artificial seed. They trick people into thinking that money and materialism is God's mechanism of influence. Money is never a substitute, representation or metaphor used to describe the word of God.

The Rosetta Stone

In 1799, the French discovered a stone in Rosetta, Africa that was originally created in 196 BC. The Rosetta Stone is an ancient Egyptian artifact that helped in the advancement of understanding various historical writings. Revelation from God is what Christians need to understand the Bible. Otherwise, misunderstood words can confuse believers instead of offering enlightenment. Words possess a phenomenal source of power. Words influence, persuade, captivate, liber-

51

ate, motivate, deceive and inspire. Words ignite wars, set standards, portray principles, characterize cultures, define doctrines, and have the potential to empower or imprison—even people. With words, we bless or we curse. Words will build up or break down. Words cause compromise or confrontation. Hence, we have the great debate about the word of God. Most scholars argue that the original meaning of many scriptures is lost in the Latin translation from Greek and Hebrew to English. However, what actually enables believers to understand God's word is revelation, not observation, interpretation, education or translation. When we diligently seek to understand the Bible, God reveals himself. On the contrary, the devil confuses Christians and nonbelievers alike, because most people simply fail to study the Bible.

In the Beginning

The Bible cites numerous propelling scriptures about God's identity. *"In the beginning was the word, and the word was with God, and the word was God"* (John 1:1). *"By the word of the Lord were the heavens made; and all the host of them by the breath of his mouth"* (Psalms 33:6). *"The Lord gave the word; great was the company of those that published it"* (Psalms 68:11). *"A word fitly spoken is like apples of gold in pictures of silver"* (Proverbs 25:11). *"But the word of God grew and multiplied"* (Acts 12:24). *"For the word of God is quick, and powerful, and shaper than any two-edged sword, piercing even to the dividing asunder of soul and spirit, and of the joints and marrow, and is a discerner of the thoughts and intents of the heart"* (Hebrews 4:12). *"Being born again, not of corruptible seed, but of incorruptible, by the word of God, which lives and abides forever"* (I Peter 1:23). *"And he was clothed with a vesture dipped in blood: and his name is called the Word of God"* (Revelation 19:13). Mankind is made in God's image and likeness. Therefore, our words carry more weight than imaginable (see Proverbs 18:21).

God Reveals

The Bible is no ordinary book. It must be approached with a spiritual perspective. The Bible uses visible experiences to describe invisible principles. Without considering scriptures in the proper perspective, the 66-books of the Bible are misconstrued and misinterpreted. Carnal-minded individuals are unable to comprehend the meaning of holy scriptures. One gospel writer describes the ability to understand revelation as a mystery. *"Unto you it is given to know the mysteries of the kingdom of God: but to others parables; that seeing they might not see, and hearing they might not understand"* (Luke 8:10). Therefore, many people read Bible verses and stumble backward with no understanding. Some readers blindly navigate into pits of false doctrines. For example, Christians without revelation actually believe that Jacob physically wrestled with an angel—they even claim that he won. Upon careful consideration, that concept contradicts other scriptures. The only way to understand the significance of Jacob's experience is to focus on the spiritual encounter, not the physical perspective. The Apostle Paul's letter to Ephesus states, *"For we wrestle not against flesh and blood, but against principalities, against powers, against the rulers of the darkness of this world, against spiritual wick-*

edness in high places" (Ephesians 6:12). The Bible does not contradict itself. Many readers simply do not have revelation. If you cross-reference multiple scriptures, none of them will contradict the other, unless you have no revelation. As well as, God's spoken word never contradicts his written word. Revelation is not optional for people who want a healthy relationship with God. Depending on God to reveal *Truth* is a basic requirement for believers. Only revelation enlightens our understanding of the Bible.

Jacob Didn't Physically Fight God

Let's consider the Hebrew word wrestle, which means to sway, as in persuade, or vibrate. Jacob prevailed, which translates as he was persuaded (see Genesis 32:22-32). He operated in fear, until he became fully persuaded of the promises of God. Perhaps you're not convinced yet. Much like Jacob's experience, it is important that you are fully persuaded. You're probably wondering why Jacob's thigh was out of joint, especially considering the theological claim that there was no hand-to-hand combat. According to tradition, God's first family, made vows by kneeling and touching the thigh of another person (see Genesis 24:2-3, 47:29). Some people say chivalry is dead. However, many men still kneel on one knee, stretching out their hand, while asking, "Will you marry me?" Vows were made similarly throughout the OT. Isn't it interesting, even exciting to know that the Prophet Habakkuk writes, *"And God's brightness was as the light; he had horns coming out of his hand: and there was the hiding of his power* (Habakkuk 3:4). The power of the Lord is hidden in his hand. Therefore, one spirit-filled touch from God opens blinded eyes; it enables those who run in fear to walk by faith. God is not trying to harm us physically; he desires to heal us spiritually. The prophet Jeremiah says, *"For I know my thoughts that I think toward you, says the Lord, thoughts of peace, and not of evil, to give you an expected end* (Jeremiah 29:11). As a child, it is difficult to comprehend how rubbing alcohol causes extreme pain in order to prevent infections. As such, God's aim is to make us better. Consider Jacob's lack of integrity. His name means trickster or he cheats. Perhaps you've heard the expression *rotten to the bone?* It comes from Proverbs 12:4. Based on the Bible, bones represent integrity. Jacob's broken bone is nothing more than a physical display of his own lack of integrity. In fact, during this same experience, God changed his name from Jacob, *one without integrity*, to Israel, which means *God heals*. It is always important to search for spiritual significance. Such careful introspection is considered too deep, in some religious circles. However, we should silently seek God's glory in everything. Instead, too many religious leaders, and legalistic Christians, exercise bad judgment when they become judgmental. Exposing *Truth* does not require indignant insults. Self-righteous Christians who publicly scrutinize others with slanderous opinions overlook the reality that God loves everybody. He draws people by loving-kindness (see Jeremiah 31:3, Luke 6:35, John 13:34-35, I Corinthians 13:13). Instead, too many Christians are so focused on hating the sin, that we forget the importance of loving the sinner. Remember, we do not wrestle against flesh and blood. As a result of fighting the wrong battles, immature churchgoers turn hurting people away from Christianity. It is critically important that we focus on the spiritual, in order to overcome the physical (see Galatians 6:1).

Bad to the Bone

Half truths are always whole lies. Therefore, instead of guessing at answers, we should rely on God. Revelation from God allows us to see things from his perspective. When God reveals *Truth* it changes the way we view ourselves and others. For instance, Jacob's experience at Peniel had everything to do with an identity change. The added value of this spiritual encounter has nothing to do with a physical battle. Prior to this experience, Jacob was bad to the bone—he had no integrity—no spiritual backbone in order to walk by faith. Afterward, life took on new meaning. Throughout the Bible, God breaks barriers so that we can experience spiritual freedom. According to Hosea 1:5, he breaks bows. He also breaks pitchers (see Judges 7:20). In order for us see spiritually, he breaks physical yokes (see Jeremiah 28:10-11). God does not meaninglessly break things or allow them to be broken. Consider the process of a crucifixion. The body is nailed to a rugged-wooden cross. The accused are usually crucified upright. Lower body strength enables such individuals to reposition themselves to survive. They use leg support to push their bodies upright for short breathes of oxygen. For this reason, the final process of a crucifixion requires breaking both legs. Soldiers broke the bones of the two thieves crucified on the left and right of Christ. However, not one bone in Jesus' body was broken (see John 19:32-33). Jesus is the word of God in human form. Therefore, he was a man of great integrity—he carried the cross bearing the sins of the world. Believers who obey God's word also live a lifestyle of integrity. On the other hand, God broke Jacob's bone in order to transform his identity (see Genesis 32:25). As Jacob, the trickster tried to avoid the consequences of death—he fled from Esau. When God changed his name to Israel, the converted con-artist received a legacy that will live forever. People without integrity are rotten to the bone. However, God has the ability to completely convert the integrity of people who chase prosperity. God wrestled with Jacob until he was fully persuaded. As a result, he changed his name from Jacob to Israel—godly integrity will change a person's spiritual identity. God is not trying to destroy us, he merely wants us to understand the importance of integrity. Poor integrity must be broken. This book is intended to help people, not ruin ministries. Integrity is merely how God prevents religious leaders from using pulpits to preach greed. The love of money will make believers bad to the bone (see I Timothy 6:10).

General Information

The Eight Primary Functions of Bones

Bones protect, provide framework, produce blood, store minerals, enable movement, protect and cleanse blood, and make-up the hearing mechanism. The word bone(s) is mentioned 101 times throughout the KJV Bible. It is important for individuals who study God's word to possess a willingness to broaden their knowledge-base. When God-chasers search for a deeper understanding of God's intentions, we gain better clarity about the Bible, life and God.

1. Protection — Bones can serve to protect internal organs. For example, the skull protects the brain and the ribs protect the lungs and heart.

2. Shape — Bones provide a frame to keep the body supported.

3. Blood production — Bones play an integral part in the blood production process.

4. Mineral storage — Bones act as storage facilities for minerals important for the body.

5. Movement — Bones, skeletal muscles, tendons, ligaments and joints function together to generate and transfer forces so that individual body parts, or the whole body can be manipulated.

6. Acid-base balance — Bone protects the blood against excessive pH changes by absorbing or releasing alkaline salts.

7. Detoxification — Bone tissues can also store heavy metals and other foreign elements, removing them from the blood and reducing their effects on other tissues.

8. Sound transportation — Bones are important in the aspect of hearing. There are three bones that make-up the hearing mechanism called ossicles. These three bones are

the smallest in the human body. They are contained within the middle ear space and serve to transmit sounds from the *air* to the inner ear. *"The wind blows where it (wills), and thou hears the sound thereof, but canst not tell whence it cometh, and whither it goes: so is every one that is born of the Spirit"* (John 3:8). As sound waves vibrate the eardrum it moves the malleus. The malleus transmits the vibrations. The absence of the auditory bones would constitute a moderate-to-severe deafening.

Exposing the Enemy

Believers must be able to hear from God in order to see what he sees. *"So then faith cometh by hearing, and hearing by the word of God"* (Romans 10:17). The battle of words began far before Jacob's experience with the angel at Peniel. According to the 12th chapter of *Revelation*, there was a war in heaven. Michael and his angels fought against Satan and his angels. This combat was not waged with physicals weapons and fists. In order to fight spiritually we must engage with God's word (Ephesians 6:17). Dragon, serpent, and snake are names of the devil. He is also called Lucifer, Satan, the father of lies, and the enemy, among other things. However, he once served as God's ministering angel with responsibility over praise and worship (see Revelation 12:3-4). Satan's reign concluded when he attempted to exalt himself above God (see Isaiah 14:12-14). Unfortunately, his tail deceived many angels who also fell from God's eternal presence. *"The ancient and honorable, he is the head; and the prophet that teaches lies, he is the tail. For the leaders of this people cause them to err; and they that are led of them are destroyed"* (Isaiah 9:15-16, also see Deuteronomy 28:13. The tail of snakes serve two purposes. The tail is where waste is released and reproductive organs are located. Satan reproduces deceptive messages. In fact, the Bible indicates that Satan is the deceiver of the entire world, church-folks included (Revelations 12:9). Even now, the devil aims to destroy his enemies with subtle and cunning words. Consider the angels that fell from heaven with him. Also consider the deception of Adam and Eve, and then consider the words that travel from your mouth. If you ever want to know what side of this spiritual battle you are positioned on, examine your words. Do your words give God glory or do they have nothing to do with revelation? As believers, we are supposed to be Satan's spiritual replacement. We will discuss the role of worship in the life of a Christian throughout this book. God has given us the responsibility of praise and worship (see I Peter 2:9). Therefore, Lucifer is furious.

Quantum Leap

When we speak words, our vocal chords vibrate. Afterward, sound waves transmit into the atmosphere. Sound is a powerful source of energy that travels at 770 mph. Our words are amazingly powerful. Scientists have even discovered how to break the sound barrier. To put things in perspective, nothing travels faster than light. Light travels more than 670 -million miles per hour. According to physics, anything that travels faster than the speed of light enters into a realm of infinity. The light of infinity is another way to describe eternity. *"For as the lightning comes out of the east, and shines even unto the west; so shall the son of man be"* (Matthew 24:27). The word is the light (see John 1:4). Only God's word is eternal. Idle words produce the kind of negative energy that travel at the ordinary speed of sound. They remain trapped in our atmosphere. The Bible refers to idle words as meaningless, gossip and negative (see I Timothy 5:13). As Ambassadors of Christ, we should speak on God's behalf. When we respond to God's intentions, our words produce extraordinary results. For example, Satan's fall from God's eternal presence was at the speed of light. *"And Jesus said unto them, I beheld Satan as lightning fall from heaven"* (Luke 10:18). When we speak God's intentions an accelerated supernatural impact always prevails. The word of God is described as being quick and powerful, sharper than any two-edged sword (see Hebrews 4:12). Light or lightning is the quickest and most powerful energy source known to exist. When we speak God's word we produce results that are out of this world, literally.

Acquitted or Condemned

The Bible indicates that heaven and earth will pass away, but God's word will not (see Luke 21:33). God's word is so quick and powerful that it transcends the barriers of space and time, entering and exiting eternity (see Daniel 10:12, Hebrews 4:12). A songwriter once sang, "I dare not trust the sweetest phrase, but wholly lean on Jesus' name." Opinionated words, despite how fluent, articulate or intriguing they sound have physical boundaries. The gospel writer, Matthew, records an account of religious leaders accusing Jesus of being Satan. During Jesus' passive response, he concludes by saying people will give an account for every idle word one speaks (see Matthew 12:36). Words are energy created by force. According to the First Law of Thermodynamics, energy cannot be created nor destroyed, only transferred. God transferred energy into mankind by breathing. Satan is aware that spiritual-beings have the ability to transfer power. Your life is valuable. Humans have worth. Despite the enemy's effort, all power will once again be transferred and apprehended by God (see Revelation 19:13). Upon the return of his son, God will permanently bind the works of Satan. The energy that is at war with God's kingdom will be transferred and trapped in the Lake of Fire. Either we will be condemned by our words or acquitted by the word of God.

Confused and Misled Church Folks

When preachers only understand fragmented facts about the Bible the devil attacks. He causes half-truths to sound authentic. It is extremely easy to focus on powerful personalities. Such listeners are often carried away by fancy sentence structures. When the truth is tainted with a teaspoon of deception results are always dangerous. People who do not study their own bibles suffer poisonous affects. *"A little leaven leavens the whole lump"* (Galatians 5:9) Ultimately, Lucifer wants to be magnified. Unfortunately, the devil is exalted whenever people are reactive to circumstances without being proactive in God's word. The Apostle Paul says, *"Study to show thyself approved unto God, a workman that need not be ashamed, rightly dividing the word of truth"* (II Timothy 2:15). On several occasions, my wife and I have misunderstood one another. As such, the author of confusion caused temporary conflict in our marriage. In effort to resolve conflict, explanations are in order. We understand the spiritual significance of eliminating ill thoughts immediately (see I Samuel 18:9-10). Otherwise, when couples allow ill feelings to linger overnight, a simply solution becomes a spiritual stronghold. *"Be ye angry, and sin not: let not the sun go down upon your wrath"* (Ephesians 4:26). It is not unusual for one of us to feel ashamed after we have gained an accurate understanding. Likewise, when we fail to comprehend God's intentions, the author of confusion causes division. As a result, we find ourselves further away from *Truth*. When people fall-in-love with God, and thirst after his word, they are willing to die for revelation. Simply said, revelation is God's way of revealing himself. Without revelation, we are spiritually blind, unable to identify God's intentions. What we see with our natural eyes is not enough. In fact, visual images are often deceptive—they are merely optical illusions. Very few people possess the revelation of Jesus Christ. *"He was in the world, and the world was made by him, and the world knew him not"* (John 1:10). Satan uses the Bible to confuse and mislead people with deception and lies. Even Christians who claim to know God, but have no revelation from God, reproduce the devil's message. Hence, so many Christians think they worship God, but they do not. Their religious routines are meaningless. They are nothing more than blinded and powerless prosperity seekers who worship and serve creation more than the creator (see Romans 1:25). Too many believers are like the Samaritan woman who met Jesus at Jacob's well (see John 4:22). They do not exalt God because of who he is, only for what they expect him to do. They seek after financial prosperity, physical pleasures and material possessions that perish. So shall the end be for those who chase after that which is perishable (see Philippians 3:19).

Knowledge is not Power

Contrary to popular belief, knowledge is not power. It sometimes produces powerful results, but it is certainly not power. Knowledge is a by-product of information. Information is gathered through careful observation. Unfortunately, observation only produces interpretation. This mind-jogging process is called education. The highest form of learning is application, but even education cannot prepare you for eternity. Education is indeed important to secure economic empowerment. However, revelation is the only way Christians can understand God's intentions. We must diligently seek God until he reveals his identity. Sunday sermons are only appetizers. God-chasers consistently pant after his presence. There are no shortcuts when accessing the glory of God. When the seven sons of Sceva attempted to cast out an evil spirit in Jesus' name, they failed. *"And the evil spirit answered and said, Jesus I know, and Paul I know; but who are you"* (Acts 19:14)? God wants to empower people who hunger and thirst for relationship. The word of God should serve the most significant role in our daily lives. Jesus instructed us to pray, *"Give us this day our daily bread"* (Matthew 6:11). Instead, prosperity seekers focus on "heaven on earth," making a mockery of spiritual things. God wants us to pray for spiritual government to rule on earth, not for corruptible currency to replace an incorruptible kingdom. Physical prosperity is not heaven on earth, but spiritual dominion is. Jesus is the word made flesh, biblically referred to as the bread of life. We are empowered when we become one with God by partaking of his word. This is the true meaning of communion. We consume God's word to survive. Afterward, thriving spiritually is the only thing that seriously matters to God chasers.

Who Wants to be a Millionaire

Study your Bible. Too many Christians are satisfied, even thrilled, with materialistic sermons. Prosperity preachers always avoid certain scriptures. They misquote the Bible and ultimately misrepresent God. Therefore, so many churchgoers are eagerly waiting to get rich. Your attitude and confession about wealth will cause God to reject you. *"So then because thou art lukewarm, and neither cold nor hot, I will spit you out of my mouth. (17) Because you say, I am rich, and increased with goods, and have no need of nothing"* (Revelation 3:16-17). When our affections our set on physical possessions, and we claim to be spiritually focused, we become lukewarm. *"Set your affection on things above, not on things on the earth"* (Colossians 3:2). Too many Christians misrepresent God's kingdom. It is not a physical kingdom. The kingdom of God is a spiritual domain. God's plan for provision always starts with spiritual

65

fellowship and assignment. It is impossible to serve God and money (see Luke 16:13). The blessings of the Lord makes us rich in God's word, not this world. Most people mistake spiritual prosperity for physical wealth. The two have nothing in common. God does not want Christians gleaning from millionaires, he wants mankind to treasure the truth (see Matthew 6:19).

Money is an Illusion not the Solution

Rich people indeed have one advantage over the poor. They unequivocally understand that money is not the answer to their unsolved problems. *"Better is little with the fear of the Lord than great treasure and trouble therewith"* (Proverbs 15:16). The devil uses deception to distort the Bible, causing confusion and preying on the physical desires of people like you and me. Therefore, he prevents prosperity preachers from saying, *"For the love of money is the root of all evil: which while some coveted after, they have erred from the faith, and pierced themselves through with many sorrows"* (I Timothy 6:10). Faith enables us to focus spiritually. This is why we walk by faith and not by sight. Faith is not some secret ingredient to enhance get rich quick schemes. *"And having food and raiment let us be therewith content"* (I Timothy 6:8). When people focus on distractions like money and pride, they are easily misled. Perhaps we've overlooked the scripture that says Jesus had no home to lay his head. Now-a-days, the highlight of most Sunday morning sermons is money. Such sermons are centered on the theme of new homes, luxury cars and large bank accounts. Nothing is evil about a new home, luxury car or a large bank account. However, theology is the study of God, but financial prosperity is based on physical wealth. Some prosperity preachers hold to fallacious fact that physical wealth is a means by which God establishes his covenant with man on the earth (see Deuteronomy 8:18). However, the new covenant was accomplished by the crucifixion of Christ. An immaterial God will never establish his covenant with corruptible possessions (see Psalms 49:6). Many churches go astray when they use wealth to measure God's validity. Money does not make the world go around, God does, literally.

Treasure the Truth

Jesus fed thousands of followers with limited resources. He used prayer, not money. Jesus didn't rely on his treasurer, Judas. Money is not the solution for people who desire miracles. Neither does it spark God's interest when you give money hoping for a spiritual encounter. Countless churchgoers have been conned and cheated. When we trip and fall based on lustful obstacles we only have ourselves to blame. Stop relying on earthly treasures and learn to treasure the truth. Prosperity preachers haphazardly persuade people, primarily those with socioeconomic struggles. They capitalize on Christians who consistently fail to study their own bibles. *"For thus says the Lord, Ye have sold yourselves for nothing; and you shall be redeemed without money"* (Isaiah 52:3). Giving is good when wisdom is applied. We should care for others. However, we should not give with secret and selfish ambitions of manipulation. *"Let no man seek his own, but every man another's wealth"* (I Corinthians 10:24). These are scriptures that the prosperity theology intentionally disregards (see Appendix D: *The Truth About Financial Prosperity*). Giving to get more money in return contradicts what the Bible actually teaches about giving. It is more blessed to give than to receive (see Acts 20:35). We should never give expecting to get more money in return. God does reward cheerful givers. However, he gives spiritual gifts, not physical possessions. On the other hand, the devil has deceived so many dreamers into thinking that physical prosperity is God's answer to poverty. Poverty has more to do with a state-of-mind, not a condition of lack. Jesus gave the rich young ruler a revelation about personal assets. *"And Jesus said unto him, The foxes have holes, and the birds of the air have nests; but the Son of man hath not where to lay his head"'* (Matthew 8:20). Jesus was homeless, but not impoverished. Poverty is based on a mentality that money will never impact. Greet the poor with the gospel and gain expected results. Remember, faith did not produce physical possessions for the King of kings himself. Even still, prosperity preachers promise listeners houses, jobs and cars. In response, parishioners sow financial seed hoping for physical blessings. This is not God's plan. When the rich young ruler realized just how spiritual-minded Jesus was, he walked away sadly. It is difficult for people to forsake physical aspirations. Faith is indeed God's answer to anything we lack. However, faith is not physical, and neither does it produce physical results. Faith is the invisible substance that gives proof to a spiritual kingdom. Faith is like the wind, you cannot see it, but there is evidence that it exist (see Chapter 4: Proof of Promises Eyes Cannot See). *"For we walk by faith, not by sight"* (II Corinthians 5:7). proven to exist. Faith allows us to see our expected end. *"But wilt thou know, O vain man, that faith without works is dead"* (James 2:20). Faith demands a response. The process is as follows. We hear God's word, and then our faith is increased. Afterward, God expects us to do something about what we see. People who see what God sees, and do nothing about it or turn a blind eye, die spiritually. We must do something about the injustices that God has allowed us to see. Unfortunately, new-aged prosperity seekers are magnetically drawn to physical aspirations. They esteem perishable possessions and ignore the eternal promises of God. Jesus said, *"Take no thought for your life"* (Matthew 6:25). Treasure *Truth.*

Stop Weeping and Do Something

Jeremiah is known as the weeping prophet. In addition to the book of Jeremiah, he also wrote Lamentations. Jeremiah is well-quoted in Christian circles for the following expression. *"But his word was in mine heart as a burning fire shut up in my bones"* (Jeremiah 20:9, also see Lamentations 1:3, Ezekiel 24:10). Remember, this chapter has a lot to do with biblical integrity. In essence, God gave the prophet Jeremiah visions about the wickedness in Israel. He saw visions in the spirit-realm that caused an initial response of passionate wailing. He desperately wanted to ignore God. According to the Bible, the prophet wanted to stop making mention of God. People who see spiritual visions from a physical perspective also fail to focus on the cross of Christ. However, Jeremiah concluded that God's word is like fire shut up in his bones.

In other words, Jeremiah's integrity would not allow him to ignore what God showed him. Far too many Christians are afraid of conflict. Instead of confronting the wayward ways of blindsided leaders, they complain amongst their peers. Instead of rallying against the wicked deeds of evil men and criminals in society, people gossip, backbite and complain amongst themselves. We can no longer bottle up our frustration and pretend as if God has not shown us anything. Much like Jeremiah's initial response, society ignores the truth and make no mention of God. Unlike Jeremiah, they fail to demonstrate integrity. Don't give up. Don't surrender to the devil's deception. *Fight the good fight of faith* (I Timothy 6:12). In order to have integrity Christians must have courage. Christians without courage die during spiritual battles. Remember, faith without works is dead. For instance, Eli the priest, allowed his sons Hophni and Phinehas to continue in misguided mischief. Among other things, they stole from the temple as young priests. Eli said nothing. Eli did nothing. Eli died in the same day as his two sons (see I Samuel 4:15-20). God's glory departs when righteousness is silenced. For this reason, Eli's daughter-in-law, Phinehas' wife, gave birth to a fatherless child. *"And she named the child Ichabod, saying, The glory is departed from Israel"* (I Samuel 4:21). When Churches and communities fail to combat injustices, God's glory departs. As Christians, filled with the fire of the Holy Ghost, we ought to be like Jeremiah. Where is your integrity? Never allow injustices to silence you (see Isaiah 58:1). Stop weeping about your situation and do something about it.

Chapter **3**

The Masquerade of Monstrous Men

SEEDTIME

Welcome To God's World

For various reasons, many Christians avoid the book of *Revelation*. What people don't know anything about, usually causes intimidation. Some say the prophetic book is far too difficult to comprehend. Nonetheless, *Revelation* is relevant right now. The metaphors and figurative language in *Revelation* are far more meaningful than most people imagine. At a physical glance, the account is terrifying. This is why faith is critically important. For those of us who walk by faith, the book of *Revelation* does not incite fear. It is much more meaningful than a horrifying depiction of the end of the world. It is a primary piece of a spiritual puzzle. It proves that physical experiences have the ability to cause trivial and tricky illusions. Faith enables us to envision the promises and Kingdom of God (see Hebrew 11:13). However, God's promises are not physical. The Kingdom of God causes everything we visibly see to reflect something of greater spiritual value.

Physical Pleasures Ruin Spiritual Success

Avoiding the book of *Revelation* enables the devil to easily deceive people. *Revelation* opens readers eyes to the reality of what God truly values. The central theme of Christianity is not physical gain (I Timothy 6:5-6, II Timothy 3:16). Everything written in *Revelation*, and the other 65-books of the Bible is spiritual. When we understand *Revelation*, we will understand God's creation. Mankind is the most significant aspect of creation. God breathed into man and transformed him into a living soul (see Genesis 2:7). It wasn't until the fall of Adam that mankind assumed a sinful nature. God gave his spiritual son, Adam, dominion and authority over every aspect of creation. We are made in God's invisible, immaterial and spiritual image. This is why physical possessions are not a priority for people who know their self-worth. If we seek first the Kingdom of God, or put spiritual things back in the proper perspective, everything that matters will be added to our lives (see Matthew 6:33). As sons of God, we have dominion and authority over the earth. Therefore, when we focus on spiritual things, everything that matters comes into agreement. On the other hand, disobedience to God is a direct defiance to our spiritual nature. For instance, according to the Bible, people who commit sexual sins violate their own bodies (see I Corinthians 6:18). The wages of sin is spiritual death. All sin is the result of focusing on physical things—the lust of the eye, the lust of the flesh, and the pride of life (see I John 2:16). In this world, physical things seem more important (see I Corinthians 15:46). In God's world, spiritual things always take priority (see I Corinthians 2:13). It is important for true Christians to see life from God's perspective. Unfortunately, crooked pulpit officials attempt to taint the truth. However, there are honest pastors who focus on the things that matter to God (see Jeremiah 3:15). True pastors impart knowledge and understanding about spiritual things, not physical possessions. Organized religion needs more honest leaders. This book will precisely inform believers what God expects concerning money. Meanwhile, it is important to understand the book of *Revelation*. It explains why Lucifer is so furious with humanity, and how he uses physical pleasures to deceive people.

Physical Realities are Based on Spiritual Principles

Our only guide through darkness is revelation from God. God's revealed word is the light of the world (see Genesis 1:3, John 1:4) If we expect to live as light in this dark world, we cannot hide in fear. We cannot turn a blind eye to the truth. The book of *Revelation* helps readers to realize how Satan lost his place in Heaven. We are Lucifer's official replacement. He was created for praise. Now, God desires to inhabit our praises (see Psalms 22:3, I Peter 2:9). The book of Revelation marks the place where everything that is good spiritually triumphs over evil. Satan is the evil one. The Bible references him as the idol god of this world (see II Corinthians 4:4). This world is physical. This is why we must set our affections on the true Kingdom of God. *"Set your affection on things above, not on things on the earth"* (Colossians 3:2). We are physical beings engaged in spiritual warfare. As spiritual-minded believers, we are more than conquerors. During the Gulf War, many of my buddies were wounded, and others were killed despite sophisticated weapons of warfare. So-called Christians, who rely on physical tactics and resources suffer loss. As a born again believer, the weapons of our warfare are not carnal (see II Corinthians 10:4). We cannot combat Satan with financial prosperity. He tricks passionate people into fighting spiritual poverty with natural resources. If we attempt to do so, we will lose. The devil is invisible.

74

Trying to combat an invisible force without the shield of faith is like fighting against the wind. God does not want us to be worn out by Satan's schemes. When believers study the Bible, it transforms our way of thinking. The book of *Genesis* undoubtedly marks the beginning of this physical world. However, the book of *Revelation* marks the beginning of a new heaven and a new earth (see Revelation 21:1). Despite the chronological order of the 66–books of the Bible, *Revelation* serves the most spiritual significance. As a consequence, people who focus on physical things do not understand spiritual principles. If Christians fail to exercise faith, we will never understand what matters most.

Beware of the Devil's Advocate

The Bible denotes Satan as the author of confusion, the deceiver of the brethren, and the father of all lies. He is a thief on a mission to steal, kill and destroy (see John 10:10). The prince of this physical world uses secular things to secretly accomplish his evil deeds. The purpose of this section is to expose Satan's strategy. According to the 13th chapter of *Revelation*, the anti-Christ will arise out of the sea. As you are aware, a sea is a large body of salt water. The elements that make up various salts, such as chlorine and sodium, start out as rock. Therefore, without revelation from God, Christians cannot serve as the salt of the earth. Water and acid erode rocks, and then rivers carry the elements into the sea. Some salts heal and other salts kill. Salt is used as a metaphor. The anti-Christ will present himself as a healer, but he is actually on a mission to kill. Another important metaphor mentioned in the Bible is water. Water, in and of itself, is a figurative depiction of God's word. However, the anti-Christ will distort the word of God. He is the author of confusion. In essence, he misuses the Bible to bewilder, baffle and bamboozle believers. He squanders scriptures to perplex people. In fact, some sources identify the Sea of Galilee as the Sea of Revolution. Satan magnifies physical possessions to manipulate Christians into revolting against God. It is critically important to study the Bible in order to rightly divide the word of truth. The devil desires to distort God's intentions. Therefore, he uses Christians without revelation to reproduce and redistribute his mystifying message. Christians who fail to study God's word unintentionally support Satan's mixed-message and malicious mission. Likewise, people without revelation seek self-serving messages and dazzling dialogue. They are plagued with itchy ears (see I Timothy 4:3). Revelation is extremely essential. God desperately desires us to study his word. Intentions are made clear when we study literature, lessons, life and even our loved-ones. If a man studies his own wife he'll understand her intentions. More importantly, seek to understand God's intentions. Casual reading is not sufficient. God demands diligence and determination. Jesus instructs believers to seek the Kingdom of God (see Matthew 6:33). God rewards those who diligently seek him (see Hebrew 11:6). Seekers will be rewarded upon the return of the Lord (see Revelations 22:12). Our reward is not based on corruptible possessions, but eternal life. Beware of people who teach followers that physical possessions represent their heaven on earth.

Secret Chambers of the Soul

King David hid God's word in his heart. Likewise, we should hide the sacred jewel of Jesus in the secret chambers of our soul. Personal relationship with Christ is critical. There will come a time when believers will have no access to the written word, *"there will be no more sea"* (Revelation 21:1). This is why it is important to hide the treasure of God's word in the secret chamber in your soul. Some Christians claim to have good intentions, but good intentions are not good enough. Physicians with good intentions undergo malicious lawsuits because of mal-practice. Despite good intentions, people die. Couples with good intentions have gotten divorced. Friends with good intentions have become enemies. Countries with good intentions have gone to war. Revelation is the only thing capable of catapulting us into eternal life. Subsequently, revelation enables us to understand God's intentions. The devil easily deceives Christians who read their bibles and lack revelation. The devil is a diabolical counterfeit. Watch out for people that allow Satan to use them to distort God's word—Beware of the devil's advocate. He imitates Christ. As a final example, the book of *Revelation* describes Satan's strategy to counterfeit and conquer Christ (see Revelation 13:1-18). God gave all power to Jesus Christ. Satan will give all his power to a man referred to as a beast. Christ was beaten like a criminal and crucified. The beast was wounded until he died. Likewise, they were both resurrected. Counterfeits are like the real thing, except they have no value. When cashiers and bankers inspect

American currency, they are trained to look for secret inscriptions called holograms, money strips and texture. People who are unaware are unable to identify the real thing. The only way to beware of false teachers is to possess a one-on-one relationship with God. Don't focus on the physical vault that is filled with worldly value. Measure the worth of God's word and hide it in the secret chambers of your soul.

Pastors from the Pit of Hell

After the anti-Christ, another beast is referenced in the book of *Revelation*. This particular beast is described as a mortal man. The biblical metaphor used to depict mankind is dust. Hence, we understand that God formed man from the dust of the ground (see Genesis 2:7, Ecclesiastes 3:20). The beast referenced in chapter 13 of *Revelation* is described as one who comes from the dust of the earth. The anti-Christ will empower a man to deceive believers with signs and wonders (see Revelation 13:13). This is why Jesus taught his disciples not to allow visible signs to influence their faith (see Mark 8:12). People who are persuaded by signs have poor judgment. The Apostle Paul explained that signs and tongues are intended to persuade people who do not believe (see I Corinthians 1:22, 14:22). However, modern-day Christians are fascinated with miraculous visuals. This is exactly how Satan will trick people into trailing the beast (see II Thessalonians 2:3). This is also how the beast will be bamboozled by his own trickery. He will teach false doctrines and deceive others as well. Afterward, he will validate his deceptive message with signs and wonders. Satan catches his bait with promises of financial prosperity. It is easy to trap prey into a web with the right bait. Most people want money, pleasures and power. The Bible references to such desires as the lust of the eye, lust of the flesh, and pride of life. Satan specializes in poisoning people with temporary prosperity and then binding them with the cares of this world (see Luke 8:14). We cannot visibly see him because he operates in darkness. He secretly influences people, especially spiritual leaders. Some religious leaders have hundreds, even thousands of followers, but fail to realize the venom they spew (see Matthew 12:34, Deuteronomy 32:33). The weapons of wealth, pride and sexual immorality are the devil's most diabolical deception. Powerful people control money, but money controls powerless people. Contrary to popular belief, ministry does not require financial resources (see Matthew 10:6-14). On the other hand, missions do. Even non-believers support worldwide missions, but only men of faith understand the mission of ministry. The serpent easily manipulates unlearned people who arrogantly assume that money is the solution to every situation. According to *Revelation*, Satan misuses men (Revelation 13:11). If you fail to focus on spirituality he will deceive you. He misuses some apostles; some prophets; some evangelist; and some pastors and teachers. Satan does not discriminate. He even tries to seduce spirit-filled Bible-based believers. Just as believers make up the body of Christ, church leaders who teach false doctrine make up the body of the beast. The Bible references them as the synagogue of Satan (see Revelations 2:9). Christians are supposed to selflessly demonstrate the love of Christ. People who esteem perishable possessions exercise the power of the anti-Christ. *"Woe be unto the pastors that destroy and scatter the sheep of my pasture! says the Lord"* (Jeremiah 23:1). Pastors must be careful not to focus on physical possessions (see Jeremiah 23:1-17). Those who do so, surrender their true worth to the devil. Therefore, people must be mindful of the message that comes from the pit of hell.

Music to the Ears

Upon the resurrection of Christ, he possessed all power. *"And Jesus came and spoke unto them, saying, All power is given unto me in heaven and in earth"* (Matthew 28:18). The book of Revelation, chapter 13, indicates that the beast, which is ordained by Satan, soon after possessed power. Certainly Christ did not empower the serpent. Much rather, Christ empowers Christians. According the Bible, Jesus transfers power to believers (see John 1:12, Acts 1:8). It is unfortunate, that new-aged Christians measure their self-worth with personal assets. As a result, religious prosperity seekers have no comprehension of spirituality. Therefore, they trade spiritual dominion for earthly possessions. This is how the devil is empowered. He influences spirit-filled Christians to submit and surrender to his strategy. The shield of faith is what protects us from his strategic attacks. Unfortunately new-aged prosperity seekers are tricked into thinking that faith is for producing physical results. Hence, many modern-day Christians are clueless as to why they are powerless against sinful oppositions. The reason spirit-filled believers surrender to Satan is because they are powerless (see II Timothy 3:1-5). For instance, Lucifer is especially manipulative in the area of music. Words travel through vibrations. Music is a variation of vibrations that permeate within the heart. Some Christians actually believe that it is genuinely okay to allow secular influences to resonate in their soul. There are three Hebrew boys mentioned in the story of King Nebuchadnezzar (see Daniel 3:5-6). These men of faith refused to submit to pagan music, even though their lives were at risk. The three Hebrew boys understood the power of music as it relates to worship. For this reason, they were willing to be burned to death, instead of responding to the kings music. Unlike modern-day believers, Israelites clearly understood the mystery about music. Many Christians today compromise. They surrender. They transfer their power to the devil. Like Adam and Eve, these new-aged children of God do not realize the seriousness of their behavior. Neither do they recognize the seriousness of music. When David played his harp before King Saul, evil spirits were forced to flee (see I Samuel 16:23). Music has an invisible, yet powerful impact. When Paul and Silas started singing praises to God, the prison doors automatically opened (see Acts 16:25). The Apostle Paul admonished believers to sing hymns and spiritual songs (see Ephesians 5:19, Colossians 3:16). Instead, new-aged believers sing songs that satisfy the lust of the flesh, the lust of the eye, and the pride of life. Music is more powerful than carnal-minded Christians will ever know. Here in lies the power of the anti-Christ. Satan is searching for ways to transfer his influence into your life. By its nature, you will transfer your dominion into his reign. Does the music you listen to give God glory or satisfy your listening pleasures? Satan wants his message to sound like music to your ears.

The Masquerade of Monstrous Men

Remember, the second beast is called the false prophet and false teacher. He attempts to make all the inhabitants of the earth worship the first beast. Remember, Satan is a counterfeit. Unfortunately, most people don't understand the affects of deception. Likewise, many others do not believe they possess the potential to be deceived. Therefore, they remain deceived. I have several associates who claim to understand Satan's deceptive use of secular music, but they are powerless and without spiritual authority to resist. They no longer have the strength to overcome Satan's stronghold. Some of these associates are even pastors. They are convinced that music serves no spiritual significance. However, Satan knows more about the invisible effects of music than most Christians. It is easier to empathize with non-believers who can't break free from this stronghold. However, it is an utter disgrace when Christians, who are supposed to be people of faith and revelation, are mesmerized by secular music. Avoid anything that is void and without respect for God. The Princeton dictionary defines the word secular the same way pagan worship is defined—they are both void and with no respect for God. His mission is clear to those who understand the relevance of revelation. Some Christians clearly have good intentions, but good intentions are not good enough. Be on alert for people who masquerade throughout churches as monstrous men.

Power and Authority

The Bible describes three types of angels: Gabriel and the working angels, Michael and the warring angels, and Lucifer and the worshipping angels. When Lucifer decided to exalt himself above God, he was removed from heaven (see Revelation 12:9). Now the body of Christ is appointed as his replacement (see I Peter 2:9). In opposition, Lucifer is after our praise and worship. He wants to take possession of our power. The greatest distractions dominant choirs and praise teams. Satan especially despises praise leaders and people who possess spiritual authority. Considering this, choirs and praise teams have issues with drama, gossip, homosexuality, fornication and much more. Despite the angelic sound and beautiful robes, Satan attacks. Garments, like robes, are figurative of authority, as annotated in the Bible. Joseph's coat of many colors signified his royalty (see Genesis 37:3). Priestly garments were required during ecumenical services (see Leviticus 6:10). Elijah gave his garments to Elisha, which he used it to divide the bank of Jordan (see II Kings 2:14). Christians are instructed to have their lions gird about with truth (see Ephesians 6:14). The army of God is clothed in garments of fine linen (see Revelations 19:14). Even modern-day police officers, fire fighters and judges wear authoritative garments. Every believer is intended to possess a garment of praise (see Isaiah 61:3). These, among many other scriptures, make it intrinsically clear that garments represent authority. Christ is the head of the church—the one in authority (see I Corinthians 11:3). The Bible defines the difference between ecumenical and administrative services. These two components of the church doctrines enables a system of checks and balances. It supports the idea of democracy. It prevents church founders from ruling as idol gods or beasts. In many modern-day churches, pastors make every decision. They control the ecumenical and administrative aspects of the church. This is dangerous. However, in some churches, controlling deacons prevent promising pastors from carrying out their ecumenical responsibilities. This is also a disgrace. Leaders should know their roles and stay in their places. Authority has everything to do with the decisions you make. Poor decisions often result in loss of authority. For example, prison is a physical consequence of misused and abused authority. On the other hand, power is transferred through blood. The definition of the word blood is voice; to bare witness; life system; and spirit. For this reason, Abel's blood cried out from the ground (see Genesis 4:10). Praise and worship require crying out to God (see John 4:24). Hence, praise and worship has everything to do with authority as well as power. The woman with the issue of blood touched Jesus' garments and immediately she was healed (see Matthew 9:20-21). The sick woman had an issue with power. As such, she relied on Jesus' authority. Power and authority works hand-in-hand with praise and worship. Whatever you consume will consume you. If your life revolves around physical pleasures, then the idol god of this physical world is your spiritual father. True believers focus on our heavenly Father who is a Spirit (see John 4:24).

Chapter **4**

Proof of Promises Eyes Cannot See

SEEDTIME

Faith that Works

It is a shameful reality that most Christians seldom, if ever, study their own bibles. The Bible teaches us everything about life. Even still, churchgoers try to seek God based on their own superstitious pretenses and emotions. For this reason, we've included this chapter to help readers recognize how the idol god of this world blinds believers (II Corinthians 4:4). Just like Satan tempted Jesus in the wilderness, he will tempt you in this physical world. The devil attacks spiritual identity. "If you are the Son of God," and "For it is written," are examples of how the devil attempts to manipulate men and women (see Matthew 4:1-11). Unfortunately, we've been tricked by childhood nightmares and horror movies. In reality, Satan is not a midnight monster intended to scare us. He allures people—he doesn't chase them away. There is a difference between fear and fright. Satan wants us to cower in fear, instead of walking by faith (see Hebrews 10:38-39). Therefore, he distorts the true meaning of faith. Frightened people are merely afraid of illusions. This chapter will introduce you to a life-changing principle. It will enlighten you about a powerful scripture that most believers have memorized, Hebrews 11:1. It will probably contradict everything you thought you knew about faith. In 1987, secular artist George Michael recorded his hit song, *Gotta Have Faith*. The faith he describes has nothing to do with the biblical explanation of faith. It is natural to hope for the best, even non-believers are often optimistic. However, the faith referenced in the Bible is based on spiritual principles, not physical aspirations. This chapter will teach readers how bib-

86

lically-based faith works.

Understanding How Faith Works

"Now faith is the substance of things hoped for, the evidence of things not seen" (Hebrews 11:1). Most readers error when verbally reciting this scripture. The word "and" does not exist anywhere in this text. The sentence is an expression of one complete thought with only one premise. Most readers say, "substance of things hoped for *and* the evidence of things not seen." This error grammatically implies that faith is two-fold. On the contrary, accurately stated, the comma suggests that the first part of the sentence is a fragment. Sentence fragments are not complete thoughts. Faith is the substance of things hoped for. Not in addition to, but simultaneously, it is the evidence of things not seen. In other words, the substance of things we hope for can never be seen with the natural eye. Faith is the substance of spiritual things already in existence, not the guarantee of physical things people hope to manifest. Faith is not intended to produce physical results. Faith is proof of unseen substance. If you can see it, faith did not produce it. Therefore, faith does not result in houses and cars. Physical examples are shadows that describe how faith works. An earthly description of faith is based on things like oxygen, carbon monoxide, magnetism, viruses and heat. These invisible entities can resurrect, kill, attract, attack and comfort. *"But the Comforter, which is the Holy Ghost, whom the Father will send in my name, he shall teach you all things, and bring all things to your remembrance, whatsoever I have said unto you"* (John 14:26). These earthly examples are terres-

trial illustrations of God's celestial glory, because scientist have proved these substances physically exist. The affects are felt, but we still cannot physically see them. Even pain cannot be seen when the effects are felt. This is how and why Jesus raised the dead, conquered the enemy, drew men to himself, attacked demons and healed the sick. Faith has everything to do with the evidence of things not seen. Similarly, faith allows us to witness spiritual things. Faith enables us to visualize life from God's perspective. Contrary to what is taught in most churches, faith is not magic. If we see what God sees, then we are protected from our invisible enemy. Human-size shields protected ancient warriors during fierce battles. The Greek word for shield means large as in door-shaped. It is derived from a word which means portal or entrance. A portal is a corridor into another dimension. For instance, to see images displayed on the worldwide web, computer users must travel through various portals. The shield of faith is a dimension where we see spiritual things. Faith is our shield. According to scripture, sight is more important than any other weapon of spiritual warfare. *"Above all, taking the shield of faith, wherewith ye shall be able to quench all the fiery darts of the wicked"* (Ephesians 6:16). Unfortunately, when people fail to understand how faith works, they misconstrue God's plan of salvation. As a result, many Christians are twice dead (see Jude 1:12). Even so, *"faith without works is dead"* (James 2:20). When people see injustices and do not have integrity to do something about it, they die spiritually. This is how faith works.

Reconstructing Faulty Foundations

Faith is our foundation (see Hebrews 6:1). If the foundation is faulty everything built thereon fails. There is a church called St. Timothy Community Church in Gary, Indiana. It is prime real estate located on the corner of 25th and Grant Street. However, the construction crew did not think the faulty soil would result in poor structural integrity. After nearly 20-years, leaders and members experienced something quite peculiar. The beautiful sanctuary started sinking. Despite curbside appeal, good works and wealthy parishioners, the foundation failed. Only a reconstructive process could reverse the saddening consequence of the slowly sinking sanctuary. The builders had to slowly reconstruct in order to prevent disastrous affects. The tedious reconstructive process could have caused the entire church to collapse. Perhaps you've misunderstood what the Bible records about faith. Faith is for spiritual sight. Faith is how God mobilizes believers—we walk by faith. It is the spiritual life-line for obedient Christians—the just shall live by faith. Don't allow physical possessions to blind you. It is so important that we consistently examine ourselves and re-evaluate our motives. Faith is not intended to produce physical results. Faith is the lens that enables us to see spiritual things. Faith is our foundation.

Foundation of Faith Based on Romans

Atonement: At one with God through suffering (Ro 5:11).
Charity: Demonstration of love (Ro 5:8, I Co 13:13).

SEEDTIME

Confession: Formal acknowledgment (Ro 10:10).

Faith: Proof of the invisible (Ro 10:17).

Forgiveness: Pardon as if forgotten (Ro 4:7).

Grace: Unmerited Favor (Ro 3:24, 6:1).

Hope: To expect, as in to look forward to (Ro 8:24-25).

Justification: Satisfy or qualify by bail (Ro 3:28).

Propitiation: Appease with sacrifice and expiate (Ro 3:5).

Reconciliation: Bring into agreement. (Ro 15:6, II Co 5:17).

Redemption: Recovery by payment (Ro 8:23).

Regeneration: Spiritual birth, religious revival (Titus 3:5).

Remission: Abatement resulting from diligence (Ro 3:25).

Restoration: Revival of something taken away (Acts 1:6).

Salvation: Process of saving from destruction (Ro 1:16).

Saved: Rescue from danger (Ro 8:24).

Faith for Worship

Faith is proof of the invisible. Faith only illuminates what we cannot physically see. It is the evidence of things no eyes have physically seen. The invisible forces of God's kingdom are far more substantial than physical possessions. This is why Jesus says people who focus on physical possession are not fit for the kingdom (see Luke 9:62). Our vehicles, homes, unexpected checks, and other material possessions are not products of faith. To make matters worse, this is actually how Satan secretly allures people into sin. God is a Spirit, and he commands us to worship him in spirit and in truth. On the other hand, the devil is the idol god of this physical world, and countless Christians unknowingly worship him for physical results. This is what we call misdi-

rected faith. Carnal-minded Christians are completely un-
aware that they actually worship the idol god of this physical
world. Jesus said, *"You worship you know not what"* (John 4:22).
Most men fail to recognize what women want. Likewise,
Christians fail to understand what actually matters to God.
He expects intimacy. Most people only view worship as an
emotional expression of lifted hands, raised voices and
closed eyes. Much rather, worship is an intimate lifestyle.
Worship affects the way we think, feel, act, react and live.
The only way to share this sort of intimacy with God is to
see life the way he does.

Faith is Our Only Connection to God

The only source of good is God Jehovah (see Isaiah 5:20).
The most influential source that opposes good is the idol
god of this world, Satan (see II Corinthians 4:4). The only
thing that directs worship to God Jehovah or the idol god of
this physical world is our faith. Do you see what God sees
or do you want what an idol *god* has? Thank God for everything, but be careful not to ask God for physical things. Our
personal beliefs and raging emotions are irrelevant in spiritual warfare. Satan tries to corner believers into making idle
confessions that have nothing to do with God's word. Our
personal opinions do not change God or the Bible. Every
physical action is a direct response to some greater spiritual
energy. According to the Bible, signs and wonders follow
those who believe (see Mark 16:17). Blinded Christians fail
to see how they actually worship Satan. This is deception at
its best. *"In whom the god of this world hath blinded the minds of*

91

SEEDTIME

them which believe not, lest the light of the glorious gospel of Christ, who is the image of God, should shine unto them" (II Corinthians 4:4). Blindness is a diagnosis of deception. As much as we enjoy physical pleasures, we must realize that God is a Spirit, and so are we. Faith is our only connection to a spiritual God. Use faith to magnify what matters to the Master.

Refocus Your Faith

The *Name it and claim it* or *Word of Faith* prosperity movement is dangerously deceptive. However, God does want believers to call things that are not as though they are (see Romans 4:7). This is God's instruction for people of faith. He empowers us as Ambassadors to represent his spiritual kingdom. Instead, many new-aged Christians focus on physical expectations. I've seen magnetic pictures of houses and cars attached to refrigerators. Many Christians post their passions on computer screensavers. Some people cut and paste magazine and newspaper images. These images serve as reminders of what they're expecting from God. Some people even drive by dealerships and newly constructed neighborhoods—they wish for what their finances cannot even afford. They appease the lust of their natural eyes in the name of faith. Remember, education is an excellent escape from economic oppression. Unfortunately, some people are clueless of how faith actually works. Notice how the Bible indicates that Satan is the author of confusion and the father of all lies. Any doctrine that focuses on physical results is misleading (see Revelation 2:14-15). Satan is distinctively described as the idol god of this physical world. This is

92

how he deceives the whole world, although his ultimate aim is not just deception (see Revelation 12:9). His sole mission is to kill, steal and destroy. You are the target within Satan's sights—he's aiming in your direction. We can only protect ourselves from Satan's attack by using the shield of faith.

The Lifestyle of a Believer

According to the Bible, we are not supposed to love our physical lives. In fact, we should be willing to die for our faith (see Revelation 12:11). Instead, too many Christians fail to submit to faith. Therefore, many believers are afraid of death. Dr. Martin Luther King, Jr. said, "If a man has not found something he is willing to die for, he is not fit to live." This does not mean Christians are not supposed to sacrifice life like suicide bombers. Instead of killing others, we should accept the threat of being martyred for standing against injustices. Jesus said, *"Take no thought for your life"* (Matthew 6:25). He also said, *"whosoever will lose his life for my sake shall find it"* (Matthew 16:25). People who are truly chasing after God, are thirsty for spiritual results. Do not focus on the physical—those who do so are easily distracted. However, it is important to know that whatever God says will happen—his word will not return to him void (see Isaiah 55:11). Hence, signs and wonders manifest as by-products. In turn, everything we visibly see has a greater spiritual significance. For example, flowers, cards and candy are romantic expressions of love. The flowers will wither, the card will fade and the candy will be consumed. However, the valued meaning behind the possessions had everything to do with love, not the by-products. People who focus on visible images, like diamond rings, new houses and luxury cars overlook the value of meaningful intentions. Learn to value God's message, instead of seeking wealth and assets from the messenger. True believers do not focus on signs and wonders (see Matthew 16:4, John 4:48). Focus on the Spirit.

Blessings are Different from Physical Possessions

During the 2008-09 economic recession, many wealthy individuals, even Christians, lost houses, cars, businesses and investments. However, God does not take away his blessings. *"For the gifts and calling of God are without repentance"* (Romans 11:29). We must be careful not to misconstrue physical manifestations or temporal possessions with the eternal promises of God (see Ephesians 1:3, Proverbs 10:22, 28:20). Otherwise, Satan will continue to cause misguided Christians to err from the faith. The idol god of this physical world, who is the devil, uses visible illusions to deceive the masses. Wealth is not a sign of God's favor. Contrary to misquoted clichés, the blessings of God do not fall upon the just and the unjust. However, God does demonstrate his love to everyone (see Matthew 5:45). If we define faith and blessings based on money and possessions, we deceive ourselves. People can work hard, invest wisely, rob, steal and kill to gain wealth. On the contrary, mortal men cannot manipulate the blessings of God. *"For the rich men thereof are full of violence, and the inhabitants thereof have spoken lies, and their tongue is deceitful in their mouth"* (Micah 6:12). God does not value what men call riches. *"Because you say, I am rich, and increased with goods, and have need of nothing; and know not that thou art wretched, and miserable, and poor, and blind, and naked"* (Revelation 3:17). Avoid worldly distractions—set your affections on things above.

Metaphors and Figurative Language

Water, light and seed are three metaphors used to represent God's word. These metaphors are used throughout the Bible. The OT expounds on physical things, while the NT focuses on spiritual things. Everything in the OT represents something more meaningful than physical illustrations. Moses divided the Red Sea physically (see Exodus 14:21). NT believers are instructed to rightly divide the word of truth spiritually (see II Timothy 2:5). Jacob used a stone for a pillow and saw visions while sleeping (see Genesis 28:11). NT believers understand that Jesus is the spiritual rock of our salvation (see Matthew 16:18). Other metaphors and figurative language is used throughout the entire Bible. It is critically important to always examine the context of language (see Appendix A, *How to Study the Bible*).

Seed of Faith

Seed is figurative of the word of God. Money is a diabolical deception the devil uses to deviate people from the truth. Prosperity preachers have fallen victim to this deception. Jesus cried and said, *"Now the parable is this: The seed is the word of God"* (Luke 8:11). Any contradiction of this truth results in

95

false teachings and false doctrines. If we say, the seed is money we describe God's word as though it is corruptible. The seed is the word and the word is God (see John 1:1). When the flock of Israel journeyed out of Egypt, God wanted the entire nation to meet him on Mt. Sinai. However, they drew back in fear when they saw the dark cloud that represented the glory of God. While Moses stood in God's presence, the tribes quickly broke off their earrings, built a golden calve, and worshipped a physical image instead of a spiritual God (see Exodus chapters 19, 32). We must be careful not to flock after teachings and doctrines that change the glory of an incorruptible God into corruptible images (Romans 1:21). If we are indeed born again, we are born of the spirit, which is an incorruptible seed. It is unfortunate that carnal-minded Christians cannot understand the language in the Bible. Therefore, they chase after physical possessions, wealth and popularity. *"Study to show thyself approved unto God, a workman that need not to be ashamed, rightly dividing the word of truth"* (II Timothy 2:15). Christians who fail to study bring shame on the body of Christ. Instead of rightly dividing God's word, they allow Satan to use them to cause division. Prosperity churches are divided based on the haves and have nots.

Fallible Faith Causes Great Gulfs

Jacob failed to visualize how to walk by faith. People who do not walk by faith cannot rightly divide the truth. There is only one way to divide God's word. Readers must measure the validity of one part of the Bible based on another. Be-

fore God revealed himself to Jacob at Peniel, Jacob operated
in fear (see Genesis 32:20-32). Without revelation, words
will always divide. Hence, there are countless Christian denominations that are divided by false doctrines. We must
seek to understand God's intentions. Seeking for spiritual
things requires reading between the lines, yet not filling in
the blanks. We must allow God to reveal what we cannot
see. Jacob did not understand the nature of spiritual promises. Whereas he divided his servants into two camps (see
Genesis 32:7). Jesus warned believers to avoid division (see
Luke 12:51-53). *"And if a kingdom be divided against itself, that
kingdom cannot stand"* (Mark 3:24). The judgment of God divides prosperity chasers from kingdom seekers. A certain
rich man, in addition to a beggar named Lazarus both died.
One went to paradise and the other went to a place of torment. The Bible gives reference to a great gulf that separated
the two (see Luke 16:19-26). Riches have nothing to do with
faith. Therefore, fallible faith separates servants from the
Master, much like Lazarus was separated from the Lord.

The Great Word of Faith

Faith is what connects us to an invisible God. *"For by grace
are you saved through faith; and that not of yourselves: it is the gift of
God"* (Ephesians 2:8). Remember, faith is our substance.
Seeing what God sees is premium. The word substance
comes from the Latin word *substania*. It literally means
standing under. As in *"under the mighty hand of God"* (I Peter
5:6). Substania is the translation of a Greek word Ousia or
Ontic. This word signifies the spiritual substance of God

that human eyes have never seen. The word Ontic describes what is there, but not based on physical properties. For example, DNA evidence is not visible to the naked eye, but crime scene investigators are able to extract samples with scientific technology. In addition, Philosopher Roger Bacon observed the common grammar of all languages. Afterward, he stated that languages share a foundation of *ontically* anchored linguistic structures. You cannot visibly see the connection between various languages. However, the fact that foreign languages can be translated is evidence of the patterns. Faith is evidence of spiritual things that cannot be physically seen. Terrestrial examples are temporal indications of celestial glory. However, here's why earthly examples like wind fail. God is not in the wind, the earthquake or the fire. (see I Kings 19:11-12, Romans 10:17). Faith does not satisfy selfish thrills. During my childhood, I was often guilty of seeing what I wanted to see. From time to time, I ignored the truth, schoolwork and chores. The consequence of my actions resulted in punishments. Temporary torture is a high price to pay for ignoring life lessons that matter most. Unfortunately, doubters who desecrate God's dynamic of faith will die. We must make a choice between God and money (see Matthew 6:24). The devil uses physical pleasures as a psychological ploy to distract us from spiritual principles. Whereas most people have little to no comprehension of the Bible. As another example, take note of the centurion who said to Jesus, *"Only speak the word."* Jesus responded, *"I have not found so great faith, no, not in Israel"* (Matthew 8:7-10). The centurion had enough insight to recognize the spiritual authority of Jesus Christ. Instead, Christians without revelation think they have some special ability to produce magical results. The word of faith is not some physical ingredient for potions and sorcery spells (see Acts 8:9-24, 13:6-8). Those who practice such things exalt themselves above the word of faith. They disobey God, because they stray from scripture and react to emotions. Disobedience is rebellion, which is as the sin of witchcraft (I Samuel 15:23). Some people have great faith and others are grand fortunetellers. Who are you?

Faith Increases Spiritual Comprehension

According to the educational philosopher, Jean Piaget, children transition from concrete to pictorial, and then abstract cognitive development stages. At some point, Christians must grow up and transition from show and tell to studying the Bible. We often learn from what we touch, see, and then read. Therefore, the substance of our faith must remain crystal clear. As believers, we must narrow our focus on the things that matter to God. Otherwise, we trespass the spirit of God (see Proverbs 15:4). Thankfully, God forgives our trespasses. If we attempt to misuse the instrument of faith we become no different from the grand warlock of worship, Satan. Faith gives us evidence of God's existence. Considering faith, we see and understand spiritual things. There are numerous accounts of faith referenced throughout the Bible. Faith enabled Abel to offer a more excellent sacrifice. Enoch overcame death because of faith (see Hebrews 11:4). Faith is intended to please God, not our flesh. By faith, Noah was warned about rain (see Genesis 7:4, Hebrew

11:7). Abraham began a journey to an unknown and unfamiliar destination by faith. Faith gave Sarah strength to believe in God's word (see Hebrews 11:8, 11). Perhaps you've thought these patriarchs of faith received their rewards on earth, but they did not. Physical things are only shadows of spiritual realities. The Bible indicates that Enoch, Noah, Abraham and Sarah died in faith, without receiving the promises (see Hebrews 11:13). Hence, we see physical signs, but faith is not intended to produce earthly promises. Faith enables us to seek something far greater than a corruptible kingdom. Through the optical lens of faith, we can embrace the Kingdom of God.

Human Intelligence Rejects Suffering and Faith

An atheist is a person who does not believe in God's existence. Atheist and prosperity preachers have something in common. Both groups refuse to accept an all-powerful God that allows people to suffer. This is the crossroads of controlling humans who try to logically define their own creator. Without faith, it is impossible for them to understand how God operates. The gospel of Luke describes such people as those who have sight, but cannot see. They hear, but do not understand (see Luke 8:10). Atheists argue against the idea of hell and suffering. They try to logically and physically rationale God's existence. God is not physical and his thoughts are not our thoughts (see Isaiah 55:9). Prosperity preachers are pinned-down in a wrestling match against physical poverty. Both groups reject the notion of suffering. They say, "I cannot accept that a loving God would cause

100

people to suffer." Our minimal tolerance for physical pain does not change God's eternal plan. *"For unto you it is given in the behalf of Christ, not only to believe on him, but also to suffer for his sake"* (Philippians 1:29). It is important to understand that suffering is intended to give us a better understanding of God. *"That I may know him, and the power of his resurrection, and the fellowship of his sufferings"* (Philippians 3:10). People who endure heartache get better or bitter—the choice is yours. *"Forasmuch then as Christ has suffered for us in the flesh, arm yourselves likewise with the same mind"* (I Peter 4:1). Suffering is worthy of thanksgiving (see I Peter 2:19,). Even Jesus himself learned obedience through suffering (see Hebrews 5:8, Romans 8:18). Until people trust in God's unseen sovereignty they will not understand how suffering produces positive affects. Challenges usually bring out the best in humanity, consider how Americans volunteered September 11, 2001 and during Hurricane Katrina. According to the Bible, suffering is how we gain a better understanding of God.

The Kiss of Life

Remember, the Greek word for worship is Kuneo. The pronunciation is not nearly as important as its meaning. It means to kiss. Worship represents an intimate connection. According to John 4:24, *"God is Spirit: and they that worship (intimately connect with) him must worship (intimately connect with) him in spirit and in truth."* Hence, worship is a lifestyle for followers of faith. The way true Christians are supposed to live is based on our ability to see what God sees. Worship is far more than a short religious experience based on physical posture. Worship has everything to do with our daily actions and attitude. True worship requires faith. When people fail to see spiritual things they fail to experience God. In fact, it is impossible to please God or even serve God without faith (see Hebrews 11:6). Faith starts with God, who is a Spirit, and it stops with God. He is the author and finisher of our faith (see Hebrews 12:2). Remember, the devil is also an author. Satan is the author of confusion (see I Corinthians 14:33). Unfortunately, prosperity messages produce object oriented ambitions. Principles based on physical realities cannot completely illustrate the spiritual principles of faith. *"For we wrestle not against flesh and blood, but against principalities, against powers, against the rulers of the darkness of this world, against spiritual wickedness in high places"* (Ephesians 6:12). God expects believers to transition from one dimension to another (see II Kings 2:11). Always utilize the shield of faith. It is impossible to share intimacy with God without it.

False Teachers Produce Evil Expectations

False teachers who say faith is intended to produce expected results deceive entire congregations. Faith does not produce anything. Faith illuminates everything. God's word is the creative force that brings everything into existence. Christians who claim to speak physical matter into existence make themselves idol gods. When Satan attempted to exalt himself to God's excellency, he was alienated from Heaven. The word produce is only mentioned one time in the entire KJV Bible. God uses the word to mock his enemies. He especially condemns those who claim they have some strange

102

faith-based ability to self-will physical things to happen. Men do not possess the power from God to produce physical results. *"Produce your cause, says the Lord; bring forth your strong reasons, says the King of Jacob (King of the trickster). 23 Show the things that are to come hereafter, that we may know that ye are gods: yea, do good, or do evil, that we may be dismayed, and behold it together. 24 Behold, ye are of nothing, and your work of naught, an abomination is he that chooses you"* (Isaiah 41:21-24). Falsely interpreted faith is always centered on the theme of gaining selfish desires. Faith only diminishes when people doubt what God shows them (see Matthew 14:26). Peter walked on water when he focused on the Spirit. When he got in arms reach of Jesus he sank. God wants us to focus on spiritual promises, not physical results. Remember, faith opens blinded eyes; it gives spiritual sight. Faith is not designed to produce physical expectations. However, signs and wonders are physical results of spiritual manifestations. Beware of false teachers who instruct listeners to focus on temporal expectations.

The Essence of Faith

It is absolutely true that we are made in God's image. It is easier to believe the truth when we look beyond physics. Our opinions do not change how faith works. If we can see it with your natural eyes faith did not produce it. Faith is proof of the unseen. Any doctrine other than this concerning faith makes the image of an incorruptible God like corruptible men (see Roman 1:23). Faith is not some cheap corruptible currency that we use to produce pleasures for life on earth. People who trick themselves into thinking faith is designed to appease the cares of this world disgrace themselves. *"By faith (Moses) forsook Egypt, not fearing the wrath of the king: for he endured, as seeing him who is invisible"* (Hebrews 11:27). Faith illuminates the invisible. This is the complete essence of faith.

Faith Empowers Believers

Faith empowers believers. *"But as many as received him, to them gave he power to become the sons of God, even to them that believe on his name"* John 1:12). When we see what God sees, we are empowered with the ability to do what God desires. Jesus described his ability to do the will of the father based on what he saw. *"Then answered Jesus and said unto them, Verily, verily, I say unto you, The Son can do nothing of himself, but what he sees the Father do: for what things so-ever he does, these also does the Son likewise"* (John 5:19). Jesus could only do, what he saw his Heavenly Father do. We can only see the invisible based on faith. Without an understanding of how faith functions, we are powerless to do anything for God. Powerless people attempt to misuse faith for acquiring possessions. Powerful people walk by faith to focus on God. *"And Jesus came and spoke unto them, saying, All power is given unto me in heaven and in earth"* (Matthew 28:18). Christians must focus and follow Jesus in order to set their sights on spiritual principles. We must examine ourselves by faith. Walk by faith. Live by faith. As the family of faith, we must allow God to empower the body of Christ to make an immeasurable impact.

Chapter **5**

Perilous Pitfalls of Prosperity Preachers

The Cost of Christianity

Christianity is one of the most powerful world influences. The Bible is the longest standing and most sold book in print. Christianity is based on the fundamental belief that Jesus Christ was born of the virgin Mary. At age 33, he was brutally beaten and crucified to redeem mankind from the consequences of sin. He was buried in a borrowed tomb, and resurrected with all power after three days. Jesus paid the price for our salvation. Now, grace is given to believers through faith. Unfortunately many churches have gone astray. They construct cult-like doctrines and become religious compounds. A recent 2009 Harris poll indicated that more Americans voted for President Barack Obama than Jesus Christ as their personal hero. This 30-page chapter is an integral pillar of *Seedtime*. It merges the theological study of chapters 1-4 with the modern-day practices of religion in chapters 6-12. Upon completion, readers will possess the power to resurrect the reputation of churches. Temporal treasures cannot remotely compare to spiritual riches, despite the view of this new-aged prosperity movement (see Romans 8:18). If modern-day churches operate with integrity they will make an immeasurable impact. We should not dangle financial prosperity between the eyes of people to allure them to Christ. Unfortunately, greed causes greater weights of oppression. *"There is (he) that scatters, and yet increases; and there is (he) that withholds, more than is right, but it tends to poverty"* (Proverbs 11:24). Poverty is a culture. It is a systemic consequence of a capitalistic society. A capitalistic society has advantages and a pitfalls. For example, an advantage is that everyone has a chance of achieving the American dream. One pitfall is that the poor often gets poorer. Pitfalls present additional obstacles for people who are impoverished. More than anything the disadvantaged need to be rescued from the mentality of poverty. This is why Jesus preached good news to the poor (see Luke 4:18). Repentance has everything to do with changing the way people think. Based on the biblical definition of poverty, poor people are individuals who lack understanding. Hence, overcoming the mentality of poverty should be a priority in every church. Religious leaders should teach congregants how to renew the minds and transition from carnal thoughts to spiritual revelation (see Titus 3:5). Instead, prosperity preachers promote wealth to gain worldly influence. God rewards those who diligently seek him, and he compensates people with wages who mix money with spirituality (see Hebrews 11:6, Romans 6:23). The Catholic church is historically known for manipulating money to manufacture world influence. For more than 1,300 years, political leaders partnered with Catholic officials to advance the prosperity of the church. Despite the sufferings Catholic leaders imposed on poor people it excelled. Pope Adrian I was thirsty for power, control, and influence. In 787 AD, he reinstituted the tithe and used religious revenue to accomplish his worldly ambitions. Pope Adrian I is no different from modern-day prosperity preachers. When people chase after money it is inevitable that they will lose sight of what matters most. Despite this truth, there are entirely too many church leaders who strip their members of human dignity. They impregnate them with materialism. When Christians are taught to focus on financial prosperity, churches give birth to dysfunctional doctrines. Meanwhile, people who are mentally oppressed are seldom liberated. We must set our sights on spiritual kingdom principles. Wealth does has the ability to physically benefit people during this short life on earth. However, Christian leaders should not use religious institutions to make money and gain secular influence.

The Theology of Financial Prosperity

Many people are participating in church services only to leave unchanged. Coincidently, the cross of Christ is no longer the prevailing theme. I once heard a prosperity preacher say, "Keep the cross as far away from me as possible." Instead, they promote their own selfish ambitions. They've micro-sized the Kingdom of God into a new-aged depiction of the American dream. However, human eyes cannot see things pertaining to God's kingdom (see Luke 17:20-21, Romans 14:17). Most often, church-goers seldom encounter Christ. This end-time prosperity theology ultimately attempts to reduce Jesus into a hustling extortionist. Jesus' message had nothing to do with money. Furthermore, God's blessings are not for sale. *"But Peter said unto him, your money perish with you, because you have thought that the gift of God may be purchased with money"* (Acts 8:20). Large dividends of money and high hopes of material grandeur are illusions. The devil uses them to convince Christians to bow down. Consider the first temptation of Christ. The devil tempted Jesus on the high mountain in the wilderness during *his* 40-

day fast. This account marks the first NT prosperity message ever preached. Interestingly enough, it was not preached by Christ. Instead, Jesus resisted and rebuked it. *"If you therefore will worship me, all shall be yours. And Jesus answered and said unto him, Get thee behind me, Satan: for it is written, You shall worship the Lord thy God, and him only shall you serve"* (Luke 4:7-8). Worship is the most intimate form of communion. It stems from the core part of our existence. Jesus overcame the devil's temptation of financial prosperity over 2,000 years ago. Now, countless churchgoers are distracted by the devil's bait. In the OT, God dwelt in tabernacles. He promised to meet us at the place of sacrifice (see Leviticus 16:2). Now, the Holy Spirit lives in the hearts of believers. The sacrifice God requires is spiritual not physical (see Psalms 51:17). God is spirit. We can only worship God in spirit and truth (see John 4:24). When animals were sacrificed under the OT covenant, something spiritual took place. Priests slaughtered specific animals, because bloodshed is sacred and spiritual. They served as a substitute for the consequences of people who sinned. Religious sacrifices have always been spiritual. A living and breathing organism is always required for worship. Money, and no other lifeless thing, is able to serve as a substitute for something spiritual. This is why the seed of Satan cannot be interchanged or mingled with the seed of God's word. One is spiritual and the other is not. OT sacrifices were considered worship because something died. In the same likeness, Christ was crucified so that we can remain in communion with God. When leaders define monetary offerings as worship, they misconstrue scripture. Worship is a lifestyle that starts with the condition of the heart. It has absolutely nothing to do with money. It is a diabolical deception of the devil when pulpit officials confuse financial prosperity with worship. *"Beloved, believe not every spirit, but try the spirits whether they are of God: because many false prophets are gone out into the world"* (I John 4:1). Remember, Satan preached financial prosperity first. People who focus on physical possessions will always encounter spiritual problems.

The Human Horror of Wanting More

The tone throughout this chapter is masculine. It is extremely difficult to break through iron curtains of intolerable deception. The devil tempts God's people with materialism, because wanting more is human nature. More importantly, discipline is the key to discipleship. We must redirect our ambitions toward wanting more of God. Financial prosperity messages psychologically stimulate false beliefs. They auction hope to the highest bidder. They leave listeners wanting more material gain. It defies contentment. My godparents, the late Benny and his widow Betty Cole, are people who separate religion from riches. Despite human imperfections, they possessed Christian character and great work ethic. They taught others to fear the Lord, live with integrity, and to enjoy life. They never manipulated anyone for anything. They lived in a lavish home, drove new luxury cars, helped others, and enjoyed life. They never misconstrued faith in God with material gain. They possessed an impressive share of wealth. They put God first, marriage second,

110

and then family, church, friends, and others—in that order. Their priorities were clear. For this reason, they lived honorable lives. All Christians should live life based on biblical perspectives. Contentment will conquer the horror of wanting excess. There is nothing wrong with wage earning individuals wanting better lifestyles. Complacency is a sign of laziness. *"But godliness with contentment is great gain"* (I Timothy 6:6). Benny and Betty balanced the principles of contentment and hard work. A life centered on physical possessions is horrifying, especially during economic recessions. Instead, follow the examples of content Christians. Fear God, live with integrity, and enjoy life.

Greed is Never Acceptable

The prosperity theology defines quality of life based on quantity of possessions. In some churches, people who give the most are esteemed the highest. This deceptive movement teaches that financial lack is based on limited faith and minimal giving. These shameless prosperity giants are proud of their accomplishments, from big buildings and crowded congregations to popularity and wealth. *"Yea, they are greedy dogs which can never have enough, and they are shepherds that cannot understand: they all look to their own way, every one for his gain, from his quarter"* (Isaiah 56:11). Only few churches seek to serve the poor, imprisoned, sick, fatherless and widowed. Instead, most giants stick their chests out and pat themselves on the back in the faces of those less fortunate. They use creative tactics and marketing strategies to allure victims into their congregations. It is difficult to see at a glance, because greed overshadows benevolence on these plantations of prosperity. Greed segregates and discriminates against the oppressed. On the other hand, Jesus preached good news to the poor and liberated the oppressed. Greedy people only see others as opportunities to advance their own agenda. *"He that (is in a hurry) to be rich has an evil eye, and considers not that poverty shall come upon him"* (Proverbs 28:22). Even worse, is the leisure inaction of churchgoers who condone these injustices. *"The just shall live by faith"* (Habakkuk 2:4). *"Faith without works is dead"* (James 2:20). True followers of Christ always stand up against injustices. They understand that people who see injustices, and do nothing, are spiritually dead. Greed is never acceptable.

God Takes Pilfering Personal

John Wycliffe was an early Catholic reformer. He was silenced for trying to help Christians read and understand the Bible for themselves. William Tyndale was also a reformer, as well as a priest and a linguist. As a result of the Catholic bishop associating Tyndale with Protestantism, he was killed. Protestants were known as heretics for protesting against Catholic doctrines. For millenniums, religious leaders have tried to prevent laymen from understanding the whole truth about the Bible. It is difficult to pilfer money from well-educated people. Giving is supposed to be an act of charity, not a mandatory requirement for religious acceptance. This book wages battle against religious oppression. Standing up against oppressors is necessary if we expect to liberate the oppressed. We understand the cost required to stand up against religious oppression. Yet, we are willing to make the ultimate sacrifice in order to liberate the captives. We believe millions of Americans will embrace the *Truth* as a result of *Seedtime*. There are 303-million Americans. Less than half attend traditional church services. According to the United States Census Report, in 2006, American churches collected $97-billion. Imagine, if church leaders systematically divided religious wealth. Suppose they gave $1-million to every American, this would only amount to about $303-million. Afterward, they could still use billions to build large monuments to themselves. Seriously, despite these statistics, materialism is not the goal of Christianity. Ministry is not the socioeconomic mission of spreading wealth. Ministry is the act of spreading the gospel of Christ. Unfortunately, pure greed perverts pure intentions. In fact, when money was haphazardly mishandled in the temple, it angered Jesus. As a result, he violently overturned the tables Afterward, he belted out, *"My house shall be called of all nations the house of prayer? but you have made it a den of thieves"* (Mark 11:15,17). People robbed God under the old covenant of Abraham (see Malachi 3:8). Now many church leaders are robbing parishioners under the covenant of Christ. Prosperity churches place strong emphasis on the tithe—even if members can't afford it. This theology is based on OT teachings about the law. The book of Malachi explains the benefits and consequences associated with the law of the tithe. This theology suggests that Jesus fulfilled every other OT law, except the tithe. Christians support the tithe out of tradition, deception, control and ignorance. God will avenge pulpit officials who use perilous pitfalls to pilfer parishioners.

The Tithe or Tied Down

Isolating specific scriptures to drive home personal beliefs is deceptive. The account of Abraham's tithe does not substantiate support modern-day principles of the tithe. The tithe did indeed surface prior to the law. However, modern day churches claim that the tithe is mandatory. Abraham's cheerful act of giving was not mandatory. As well as, Christians are in covenant with Christ, not Abraham. The law helped Israelites honor their covenant with God. Grace is what aids Christians in our covenant with Christ (see Ephesians 2:8). Lawlessness caused a curse to come upon Israelites. If they failed to follow the law they forfeited their blessings. On the other hand, the crucifixion of Christ destroyed curses amongst Christians (see Galatians 3:13). In addition, we are eternally blessed (see Ephesians 1:3). Christ gives grace, which is unmerited favor. There is nothing, whether good or bad, that believers can do to earn grace. Churches are flooded with the *all this can be yours* money messages. Truthfully, people need to hear the *seek ye first* gospel of Christ. Pulpit officials are biblically instructed to teach people how to prioritize life (see Ephesians 4:11-13). God wants us to focus on his kingdom and his righteousness (see Matthew 6:33). Instead, prosperity seekers are taught to give money, and then hope for financial rewards. Leaders who manipulate the truth share the same shame as con-artists. Whether by ignorance or by design, people who taint the

114

truth are a disgrace to churches. The poor cannot afford costly misinterpretations about financial gain. Therefore, this book will undoubtedly embarrass leaders who ruin society for quick thrills, lavish lifestyles, and to control the masses. The poor are homeless, hungry, and nearly naked. In part, church leaders who preach what God forbids are at fault. Members who do not read their bibles have themselves to blame as well.

Curses vs. Mind-Control

There are radical contradictions in the prosperity theology. Let's examine the comparison between the OT covenant of Abraham and the NT covenant of Christ. According to NT scriptures, Christ redeemed us from any curse the law had the ability to impose. Besides, we already possess all spiritual blessings in Christ (see Ephesians 1:3). On the contrary, parishioners attending prosperity churches are misguided. They make the tithe mandatory. By doing so, they claim to receive physical blessings. Others, who do not tithe, are urged of the consequences of being cursed. Some leaders manipulate members, misuse scriptures and misinterpret the context. What type of leader are you or what type are you subjecting yourself to? Do not taint scriptures until the truth becomes contaminated. Do not teach followers to give in fear. Do not make people feel forced to give in order to gain acceptance. Religious leaders who do such things rule with oppression. These dictators mingle God's word with mind control methods. Be watchful. Others simply fail to study their bibles, and are unable to rightly divide the word of

Truth. Notice how dictators rule. They control ruthlessly. They demand as opposed to asking. They govern as slave masters rather than spiritual leaders. Ultimately, they attempt to dig deep, subverting souls and stripping people of free-will. Despite these dictators, Christ gives choices (see Joshua 24:15). He encourages cheerful giving, and instructs people not to give grudgingly or resentfully. Unlike prosperity preachers, Christ is more concerned about our attitude toward giving. Jesus never mentioned any amount one should give. There are no biblical laws associated with modern-day giving. Since there is no law there can be no curse. However, there are consequences to action and inaction. There is also a difference between a curse and a consequence. Consequences naturally result from various behavior. A curse is a supernatural act of invoking evil. We can change out consequence by changing our actions. Only God can destroy the curse. Therefore, he sent his only begotten son to pay the ultimate sacrifice. Although humanity continues to experience consequences. The emancipation of slaves took place in 1863, but countless African Americans remained on plantations without wages; many sharecroppers were freed slaves uncertain about their liberties. As NT believers, we are certainly free from the OT curse of the law. Unfortunately, prosperity churches function like plantations. Slaves and sharecroppers are like the unlearned Christians who attend. Oppression has a way of stripping individuals of individuality. People with broken spirits feel unable to break free from mind-controlling leadership. For this reason, churchgoers ignore the emancipation of Christ. They remain on these religious plantations. Churchgoers plant financial seeds, and church leaders reap the immediate harvest. *Seedtime* helps readers to journey through the Bible. As readers progress, this book will thoroughly apply biblical perspectives to money matters.

Manipulating Messages to Make More Money

The theme of Christianity is not money. *How to get rich and have everything you ever wanted*, is Satan's message modernized. In fact, money is a mere illusion. Life cannot successfully be measured by money. God sacrificed his only Son so that life would become more meaningful, namely spiritual. Money does not make life valuable, but God does. When the early church was established, believers voluntarily sold their possessions, and donated the proceeds (see Acts 2:45). They spread wealth, in order to eliminate oppression. People will always feel inclined to give to certain causes. Unfortunately, in our materialistic society, greedy congregations are plagued with filthy reputations. These churches have leaders who misinterpret scriptures and manipulate people out of money. The proceeds fatten their pockets and bank accounts, but lack remains prominent amongst churchgoers. Prosperity churches thrive off large collections, but members seldom benefit. When $97 billion is collected by churches, such as in 2006, lack should not be an issue amongst churchgoers unless greed is prevalent amongst church leaders. According to the book of Acts, Christians are expected to care for one another. Unfortunately, in today's society, many tightfisted penny-pitchers feel forced to save their resources for themselves. They do so because countless churches do more damage than good. Giving away food only deals with the problem on the surface. Food shelters and soup kitchens are only temporary fixes that cause people to stay stuck in the cycle of mental poverty. They make volunteers look good. However, those who repeatedly stand in food bank lines are humiliated. They need liberation from long-term oppression. They need a strategy to escape a system of hopelessness. Stop feeding people just to say you fed them. People who pacify problems do more harm than good. Teach disciples how to fish. Help poor people climb out the slums of ghetto without even necessarily changing their physical environment. Minister spiritual meat to the homeless. Afterward, implement job training programs. Refer them to other references sources that might be able to help. Consistently remind listeners that God is our ultimate source. Make a substantial difference in somebody else's life, instead of making yourself look good. This is the only way poor people will eat for a lifetime. Spiritual leaders should help people identify the spiritual root that led to their physical circumstances. This is the only solution for permanent change. Some charitable churches actually rescue needy people during financial crisis. Be careful not to destroy human dignity when demonstrating charity. When oppressed people are humiliated, made vulnerable, and defined by lack, human dignity seems to diminish. Remember, temporary aid pacifies permanent problems. God is concerned about the oppressed. Big buildings are worthless if they do not accommodate the spiritual needs of those in attendance. Where there is no sacrifice,

118

worship diminishes. *"I beseech you therefore, brethren, by the mercies of God, that ye present your bodies a living sacrifice, holy, acceptable unto God, which is your reasonable service"* (Romans 12:1). When we measure life based on money, we devalue the worth of human dignity. The oppressed and needy become victims in such capitalistic communities. Christ cares so much that he redeemed sinners with his life. He paid the price when money would not suffice. *"For thus says the Lord, You have sold yourselves for (nothing); and ye shall be redeemed without money"* (Isaiah 52:3). Christianity has absolutely nothing to do with financial currency. Churches have bills, but church leaders must maintain integrity. Religious facilities demand resources, but we cannot manipulate faith for money. *"No man can serve two masters: for either he will hate the one, and love the other; or else he will hold to the one, and despise the other. Ye cannot serve God and (money)"* (Matthew 6:24, Luke 16:13). Christians should strive to follow in Christ's footsteps, instead of manipulating messages to make money.

The God of Money

Interestingly enough, the tithe is a prerequisite in prosperity churches. According to these churches, giving money is a prerequisite to receive blessings from God. Too many churches aim to produce a financial harvest. Prosperity churches plant so-called seeds of money, but when these seeds take root, they produce bad behavior. *"For the love of money is the root of all evil: which while some coveted after, they have erred from the faith, and pierced themselves through with many sorrows"* (I Timothy 6:10). Instead of recognizing the bait of

119

Satan, prosperity teachers describe money as though it is God's prosperity. Faith is God's only provision. Seeing what God sees is the only way to thrive. *"Where there is no vision, the people perish: but he that keeps the law, happy is he"* (Proverbs 29:18). Yet, prosperity seekers continue to depend on money instead of God. They focus on wealth more than righteousness. They protect their assets better than their relationships. They possess a covenant relationship with money. They lust after the goddess of greed. A love affair with money is difficult to keep secret. *"For where your treasure is, there will your heart be also"* (Matthew 6:21). For this reason, it is impossible to disguise your message. *"O generation of vipers, how can ye, being evil, speak good things? for out of the abundance of the heart the mouth speaks"* (Matthew 12:34). It is obvious when people value money more than God. Actions speak louder than sermons? Even during economic struggles prosperity members are expected to sacrifice money. The welfare of poor people is irrelevant based on the prosperity interpretation of the gospel. Prosperity preachers blame poverty on the fact that poor people are stingy. The Philosophy of prosperity is ruthless. Prosperity leaders only care about church growth for personal profit and greater influence. This is why poor people, especially struggling single mothers, suffer from lack while attending wealthy churches. There are indeed extremely good churches that use influence and resources to help others. They exalt God, preach Jesus, surrender to the Spirit, and care about people—without hidden agendas. Prosperity churches also have a biblical responsibility to teach members to do the same (see Galatians

6:1). We empower people by preaching about the cross (see I Corinthians 1:18). However, this wicked prosperity movement has cast a shadow over all churches. People are rightfully skeptical about pulpit officials. Churches may never live up to the expectations of those who scrutinize its good works. Although we should never stop trying (see Romans 14:16). People who give should hold leaders accountable to routine reports. Moreover, honest and transparent leadership discloses financial information to donors. Remember, charitable resources are intended to help spread the gospel. Large dividends of money lends leaders a sense of control. Money and power without accountability and transparency leads to corruption. This is how men become idol gods, and their followers suffer shamefully. Our outlook on wealth will dictate our destiny.

Lacking Love and Loaded with Lust

Some people lust after sexual pleasures. This is called the lust of the flesh. The Bible also references to another lust called the lust of the eyes. *"For all that is in the world, the lust of the flesh, and the lust of the eyes, and the pride of life, is not of the Father, but is of the world"* (I John 2:16). These are people who are not necessarily possessed with extra-marital or pre-martial sexual desires. The lust of the eyes is an ungodly passion for physical prosperity. Despite the risk, many people continue to rob, kill and steal expecting to get rich. Prosperity seekers are never satisfied. Remember, the nature of prosperity is ruthless. The root word of ruthless is ruth. I can't imagine what my life would be like without the influ-

SEEDTIME

ence of my mother, literally. Let's just say she is a virtuous
woman who lives up to the meaning of her name, Rutha.
The biblical name Ruth means satisfied. My mother's lifestyle taught me the difference between contentment and
complacency. The root word of contentment is tent. The
root of complacency is place. The children of Israel moved
the tent of tabernacles from one place to another (see Exodus 26:12). People of faith are content with what they have,
but never complacent where they are. The word content
means information or state of mind. Most modern-day
Christians do not understand the Bible. Therefore, they have
no content (information). As a result, they cannot be content (state-of-mind). God wants us to be content in every
sense of the word. On the other hand, we should always
press forward (see Philippians 3:14). Instead of becoming
complacent, we should spiritually transition from one place
in life to the next. Faith allows us to move from one dimension to another (Romans 1:17). According to the Bible, Ruth
married Boaz. His Hebrew name means lively. Content
Christians have an agreement with life. *"Not that I speak in
respect of want: for I have learned, in whatsoever state I am, therewith
to be content"* (Philippians 4:11). Remember, godliness with
contentment is great gain (see I Timothy 6:6). I was raised
on a poor industrial city called Gary, Indiana. Prior to the
1970's, Gary was populated by middle-class Americans. I
understand the valor required to gain mental victory over
poverty. Although we didn't have much, we were never in
poverty. We understood the spiritual value of life. I've been
blessed with the tutelage of selfless people. On the other

hand, when ruthless men and women rule, the oppressed suffer. Citizens of Gary suffered from racially imposed poverty during the early 1970's. Now residents suffer from religiously imposed poverty. The first African American mayor of Gary, Richard Hatcher, was elected in 1968. Disappointed Anglo Saxons moved in masses to surrounding suburbs. The urban area suffered from White Flight. State resources and political influence followed the foot-steps of wealthy white businessmen. The socioeconomic state of Gary suffered from gentrification, joblessness and despair. In such environments, the mental oppression of poverty forces people to devalue themselves and compromise their dignity. Ruthless people cause oppression, and ruthless religious leaders cause religious oppression. The Church that Christ established is intended to be a living organism—not an organization. When high hopes of prosperity become the driving force, the organism is ruthlessly suffocated. Big business perspectives will slowly smother the flow of worship. Such church services become nothing more than religious entertainment. Manmade agendas attempt to limit an unlimited God. Incidentally, God does not make pit-stops where his presence cannot take up residence. Upon the benediction, offerings are nothing more than people paying for general admission. When money is used as a catalyst, assemblies transform into heartless corrupt corporations (see Amos 5:21). The easiest way to silence members is to keep financial records secret. Whereas, members see no evil, hear no evil, and say no evil. Extortionists hide behind poor accountability. "What people don't know won't hurt them," is a common cliché. Christians must demand transparency and accountability from leaders. God certainly demands it from you (see Galatians 2:11, I Corinthians 13:3). It is painfully disappointing that many churches care about the offering more than the giver. They depend on the tithe, as opposed to depending on God. They focus on physical possessions, and turn a blind eye to God's expectations. They lust after materialism, and drain limited resources from the poor. *"There is a generation, O how lofty are their eyes! and their eyelids are lifted up. There is a generation, whose teeth are as swords, and their jaw teeth as knives, to devour the poor from off the earth, and the needy from among men. The horse-leach hath two daughters, crying, Give, give"* (Proverbs 30:13-15). These prosperity preachers go through great lengths to control their followers. They cultivate congregations that obey out of ignorance. The key word is cultivate—the root of this word is cult. Only cult leaders encourage people to blindly follow them. God gives every man a measure of faith (see Romans 12:3). In other words, God wants every man to see what he sees. Godly leadership will encourage you to do more than merely read the Bible. We must study the scriptures for ourselves (see I Timothy 2:15). Remember, upon the benediction, Christians who fail to study their own bibles, are blindsided by well-disguised con-artists. There is only one quality that signifies a true Christian. *"By this shall all men know that ye are my disciples, if ye have love one to another"* (John 13:35). The devil influences gold diggers, but God wants us to have hearts of gold. Satan's mission is to pervert our innocence. He does not want us to be satisfied with what actually matters to God.

Despite his evil efforts, faith, hope, and charity remains. Don't forget to focus on the greatest gift of love (see I Corinthians 13:13).

Prosperity Churches and Casinos

When believers fail to study the Bible, they follow man and hide from God. At some point in life we must answer the call, "Adam, where are you?" It is a rhetorical question. God already knows where we are. He wants us to examine our lives based on his word. Too many Christians examine life based on physical possessions. Hence, financial prosperity messages have made it acceptable for churches to operate like casinos. People put money in, hoping to hit the heavenly jackpot of blessings in return. However, giving is an act of charity that expects no physical reward. Instead of generously giving to help others, prosperity seekers tithe to get more money in return. Giving to get more money in return is gambling in God's house. When churches make prosperity a priority, the devil dictates the doctrine. In other words, churches that mimic this materialistic society, love pleasure more than God. Perhaps you've asked, "Why do some churches seem to produce mess and distractions? Such chaos occurs because *"the love of money is the root of all evil"* (I Timothy 6:10). As a result, immoral lifestyles discredit the integrity of churches. "Adam, where are you?" God is interested in where you are in life, not what you have. When prosperity concepts creep into the pulpit, people focus on potential gain. The prosperity movement disregards holiness (see Hebrews 12:14). Perhaps this is why millions of Americans see no worth in churches, because prosperity churches have gambled away their good name (see Proverbs 22:1).

Selfless Sacrifices Lend a Sense of Spirituality

Remember, half-truths are always whole lies. We want readers to put prosperity in the right perspective, and also understand the importance of giving. All people should learn the value of giving, despite religion. Sacrificial giving affords people an opportunity to experience unconditional love. Giving and expecting nothing in return is the most selfless act of kindness a person can display. Nazarenes are known for vows that require nothing in return. Unlike Jesus Christ of Nazareth, many Christians give for a variety of reasons. Some people are just gamblers, others are in need of income tax write-offs. A sacrifice is an act of complete loss. Sacrifice is the result of suffering for wrong-doings. Hence, Jesus became our sacrifice once and for all. Now, we present our bodies a living sacrifice unto God (see Romans 12:1). God wants our obedience. Prosperity preachers want our money. Satan wants everything you spiritually possess. He tricks believers into making sacrifices that defy God's instructions. *"To Obey is better than sacrifice"* (I Samuel 15:22). Giving enables us to exercise selflessness. It empowers us to relate to God and understand his nature. Furthermore, giving allows us to gain a greater sense of purpose. Giving generates the kind of gain that money cannot. Giving sacrificially has an undefined value that most people will never experience. When we allow evil influences to dictate how we view wealth, we become selfish. Prosperity churches make rich men *like God*, instead of making humanity *God-like*. Selfless sacrifice is the only attribute that enables us to embody our God-like image. This is why spiritual-minded people give.

The Truth about Seedtime and Harvest

When believers truly realize that we are one with God, material possessions will not be our priority. However, there is a biblical principle called seed time and harvest. We reap what we sow. Either you can sow into God's kingdom or invest in the world's system. God's kingdom is not meat and drink—it is not physical (see Romans 14:17). The secular system revolves around economics. Satan is the prince of this physical world (see I Corinthians 4:4). If a person sows corruptible things, such as money, they will reap corruption, even death. Those of us who choose to sow into God's kingdom will reap eternal life. The expression heaven on earth has everything to do with God's spiritual dominion in this physical domain. Prosperity preachers confuse people into thinking that "heaven on earth" is about houses, cars, and big bank accounts. Seedtime and harvest is a grossly misunderstood and misinterpreted principle. Therefore, we have dedicated an entire chapter to this concept. Additional information about seedtime and harvest is referenced in chapter 10, *Making Sense of Biblical Metaphors*.

Everyday Grace

Perhaps you're familiar with the definition of grace. Unmerited favor is something given to a person who is undeserving. According to the Bible, undeserving believers have been blessed with all spiritual blessings in Christ (see Ephesians 1:3). In other words, Christ gave us every blessing that grace could access. It is because of grace that God causes it to rain upon the just and the unjust (see Matthew 5:45). Since Christ gives unmerited favor, we must also acknowledge the existence of God's merited favor. Merited favor is a reward for jobs well done. Unmerited favor is to give gifts to undeserving recipients. Although grace came through Christ, God still honors hard work. The Apostle Paul said, *"I press toward the mark of the prize of the high calling in Christ Jesus"* (Philippians 3:14). A prize is a way of rewarding success. Grace is available for everybody. Rewards are only accessed by those who strive, struggle, and suffer for something greater. When Prophet Isaiah told King Hezekiah that he was going to die. Hezekiah prayed, *"I beseech thee, O Lord, remember now how I have walked before thee in truth and with a perfect heart, and have done that which is good in thy sight. And Hezekiah wept sore"* (see II Kings 20:1-6). Hezekiah did not ask for unmerited favor. He asked for the reward of walking in truth, possessing a perfect heart, and doing good in God's sight. Hezekiah asked for longer life. Notice how he requested something spiritual from God—he asked for life. His possessions could not save him. Seek the right stuff. Again, people shouldn't attend churches expecting to give in order to get. People who do such things face disappointment and failure. Some preachers manipulate parishioners, but God does not pay for pleasures. Stop selling yourself for nothing. *"For thus says the Lord, Ye have sold yourselves for naught; and ye shall be redeemed without money* (Isaiah 52:3). Believers cannot afford to dabble with double-minded philosophies. The Apostle James said, *"let not (such a) man even think that he should receive anything from the Lord. A double minded man is unstable in all his ways"* (James 1:7-8). There are several critical principles prosperity seekers need to understand about money. Otherwise, church leaders will go on deceiving listeners. Churchgoers will continue in the cycle of giving, expecting and silently struggling. People who give their money to get financial blessings in return are double-minded. Instead, we should teach people how to use everyday grace to become one with God.

Your Outlook on Money will Reveal Your Motives

Many believers still have a slave mentality. It's emotionally and psychologically difficult to escape strongholds that keep us enslaved. Nonetheless, freedom starts within. Consider how budgets and bank statements reveal a person's habits. Whatever you value the most is what you actually treasure. *"For where your treasures are, there your heart will be also"* (Matthew 6:21). The greatest way to find out what you truly believe is to examine how you spend your money. Do you pay your debtors and help others? Are you consumed with selfish desires? Solomon, the son of King David, is noted for his incomprehensible and impeccable wisdom. In the book of Ecclesiastes 10:19, he writes, *"A feast is made for laughter, and wine make merry: but money answers all things."* Let's put this quote in the proper perspective. Solomon understood that our outlook on money will reveal our motives.

SEEDTIME

You didn't actually think that money is not the solution to our problems. Money can't buy love, cure cancer, and resurrect dead loved-ones. The only way to muzzle lies that echo across pulpits is to expose individuals to *Truth*. Slandering the guilty is wicked and ruthless. Yet somehow, *Truth* must be revealed. We may not save the entire world, but we can certainly change our own reality. We must accept responsibility for the choices we've made as individuals, whether indifferent or wrong. Otherwise, even though Christ has set us free, many believers will never experience life without bondage.

Mega Manipulation in Modern-day Churches

People who are controlled, oppressed and manipulated by con-artists, have themselves to blame as well. Individuals are often led astray by the possibility of a fast break. While driving on the freeway, trying to get somewhere quicker than usual, I've changed lanes in traffic. Fast breaks into the passing lane can be quite deceptive. In retrospect, the fast lane is often filled with regrets and delays. Searching for a quick and easy hustle can result in disappointing outcomes. Notice how financial prosperity preachers prey on money. They say, "Give what you have if you expect God to bless you with more." Individuals generally become outcasts for speaking up in controlling churches. Even innocent questions are avoided by crooked culprits. Bible studies are no different from formal Sunday services, where sermons are preached and dialogue is prohibited. Any logic that sheds light on justice and *Truth* is condemned. Perhaps this is why cults are difficult to avoid. They often start off under leaders professing Christianity. Much like the 1978 account of Jim Jones, David Koresh in 1993, or Sun Myung Moon, who acclaimed himself Messiah in 2001, these men were all Christian leaders. Such men err from the faith. They contaminate followers with confusion through mind-control. They misuse the Bible for selfish ambitions. Perhaps they previously embraced *Truth*. Physical aspirations like money and power have the ability to change anybody who is not focused on spiritual principles. Some of these wayward leaders manipulate members out of money. Others control them for personal pleasures. Some even persuade entire congregations to drink poisonous kool-aid, literally. So many bold believers claim such cult-like manipulation could not possible happen to them. However, these same people give away their hard-earned wages, self-worth, and dignity to controlling prosperity preachers. Nonetheless, these control tactics turn churches into fault-finding cults that isolate themselves. They often claim to have a better understanding of scriptures, and a closer connection to God than other congregations. Their faith is centered on the teachings of one man, as opposed to the Bible. Once these members are exposed to the truth, they face an emotional ultimatum. They must either abandon fellowship with family, friends and other churches, or silence themselves.

Set Free from Casino Concepts

It is common for many Christians to reject the truth. The Bible calls these people babes in Christ (see I Peter 2:2).

They lack integrity. Since bones represent integrity, they need the sincere milk of God's word. Don't hide from *Truth*. Don't allow the lack of knowledge to destroy you. Pray that God reveals himself to you. Afterward, *Truth* will set you free. Despite 66-liberating books of the Bible, many religious churchgoers are stuck in dens of thieves. These dark dens of defeat called prosperity churches are filled with hope that has no substance. They follow fantasies and fail to experience true faith. For instance, my 3-year-old hopes to drive morning after morning in route to daycare. Extremely impoverished people hope for immediate wealth. People suffering from obesity hope to lose weight overnight. However, true hope is based on reality, not fantasy. On the contrary, faith has substance. Although faith cannot be seen, there is evidence it exists. *"Now faith is the substance of things hoped for, the evidence of things not seen"* (Hebrews 11:1). Remember, prosperity churches are like casinos across America. They both appeal to geographically impoverished regions. They market themselves to people that fantasize about escaping poverty. According to the Bible, churches are supposed to spread good news to the poor. What is good news for poor people? Poor people can repent—they can change the way they've been thinking. They can stop focusing on get-rich-quick schemes and experience the love of God. It is truly good news to embrace the promise of eternal life. Imagine living life under the mental oppression that wealthy people are better than you. Now, through faith, the poor can see things differently. We are so valuable to God that he sent his only begotten Son to pay the price for our sins—a price no amount of money could pay. There is no better news than that. Those who think otherwise, despite their financial worth, are actually wretched, miserable, poor, blind and naked (see Revelation 3:17). Unfortunately, prosperity preachers pollute this good news. They pretend as though this world is God's paradise. These shameless giants promise poor people that God will bless them with wealth if they give what they have. As a result, the rich get richer as the poor and middle-class suffer. Instead of liberating people with the gospel, prosperity churches use the Bible to oppress. In addition to ecumenical services in the sanctuary, churches are responsible for administratively reaching out into the community. Churches should help people transition from welfare to work. They should teach people how to avoid living paycheck to paycheck. On the contrary, many religious groups continue to manipulate the masses for selfish gain. This new-aged money theology does not actually work. It is a quick gimmick that only benefits people on one side of the pulpit. Therefore, many Christians continue to give, but suffer from limited resources, recessions, false hopes, and unpaid bills that result in bad credit scores? *"My people are destroyed for lack of knowledge; because you have rejected knowledge, I will also reject you, you will be no priest to me; seeing you have forgotten the law of your God, I will also forget your children"* (Hosea 4:6). Some people are so possessed with Satan's prosperity message that they refuse to change. Others ignore *Truth* for the sake of tradition. There are also those who are afraid to face fearful religious leaders. Nonetheless, people who sow the corruptible seed will reap a harvest of corruption.

This Book is not for Everybody

There is no quick fix to liberate deceived or money starved Christians from centuries of spiritual bondage. *Seedtime* is a way of escape. Further more, this book sheds *light* for millions who have been tricked into thinking that there is a monetary cost to serve Christ. Worship experiences do not require price tags and ticket sales. This book is not written for traditional churchgoers who debate God's word without studying God's word. Revelation is essential. It is not for Christian superstars who exalt themselves for fame and wealth. It is not for people who are so emotionally attached to leaders that they lose sight of *Truth*. However, it is for a generation of believers who refuse to settle for half-truths and inadequate interpretations of the Bible. It is even for atheist, agnostics, and others who are uncertain about faith. Remember, the Church that Christ established is a living organism, not an organized business. People define churches, but organizations define people. The Church is a body of believers. Additionally, a corporation is defined as a body of people, but not based on spiritual beliefs. Corporations have a mission of financial gain. Find out why so many people are trapped in organizational bondage, even though Christ has set every captive free. This book is merely a declaration of our freedom. It utilizes OT and NT Bible scriptures to place biblical facts in the proper context. It explains how God uses provisions to advance his people, and the devil misuses materialism to tempt all people. It is unfortu-

134

nate, but preachers depend on people for provisions, instead of God. God uses all of creation—people, animals, and everything else (see Romans 1:20). However, when preachers pressure people for the tithe and offerings, they make men and women their source. When people surrender to such foolishness, they make preachers their idol gods. God wants every believer to be fully persuaded by *Truth* (see Acts 18:4, Romans 4:21, 8:38). God will use this book to change or challenge orthodox thought-patterns of prosperity churches. This book is for people whose minds have not become incurably contaminated with the poisonous venom of prosperity messages (see Jeremiah 30:12, Micah 1:9). Ultimately, this book is intended for individuals who are interested in having a closer encounter with God.

SEEDTIME

Chapter **6**

Memoirs of Merchants

SEEDTIME

Something More Meaningful Awaits You

The devil tempts people with physical pleasures, deceptive promises and financial prosperity (see Matthew 4:3-10). Satan tried to trick Jesus into turning a stone into bread, and he continues to trick Christians into trading spiritual promises for physical pleasures. He also tried to manipulate Jesus with suicidal thoughts of jumping off a cliff, and he continues to oppress believers with false interpretations of the Bible. Finally, he tried to cunningly persuade Jesus to worship him for physical wealth. His scheme causes churchgoers to chase the possibility of prosperity everyday. He distorts the true meaning of the Bible. Jesus' wilderness experience illustrates how to overcome Satan's deception, lies and confusion. People who are persuaded by the devil's plans live in darkness. Believers who diligently study the Bible walk in the light. *"Thy word is a lamp unto my feet, and a light unto my path"* (Palms 119:105). Light enables navigators to maneuver to meaningful destinations. Even when dismal light reflects on objects in dark places silhouettes appear in various shapes and sizes. These images, sometimes still, often set in motion are called shadows. Have you ever thought to yourself, "There has to be something more meaningful about religion than just going to church week after week?" Well, there is. However, many adults die before walking in their destiny. As children, we're often intrigued by shadows, sometimes even afraid. Short-lived and ever-changing shadows are clues that something is set in motion. Shadows frequently appear much larger than the objects they actually reflect—although shadows are less meaningful. The dimmer

138

the light the larger the shadows. In absolute light there are no shadows. When we walk in the light, we avoid meaningless obstacles. Shadows are also viewed as protection in Hebrew cultures. Desert travelers often seek rest under shade trees to shield themselves from the hot sun. Likewise, most people seek protection in meaningless material possessions. Sometimes reality is difficult to withstand. Especially considering how God's word purges people of worldly passions. The NT is evidence that the OT law was a shadow of things to come (see Hebrews 10:1). All 66-books of the Bible are equally important. The Old and New Testaments compliment one another. The NT is merely more meaningful to modern-day believers. However, Christ did not destroy the law, he came to fulfill it (see Matthew 5:17). Think of it this way, Christ sheds light on the OT. True Believers acknowledge the worth of the entire Bible. They seek to appreciate its context and study to understand its meaning. God's word is like an extended love letter intended to touch the hearts of those who desperately desire intimacy with him. Unfortunately, clueless Christians fail to study and others simply haven't taken the time to learn how. Consequently, they live in darkness without protection, possessing no comprehension about spiritual principles. They seldom fulfill their purpose. Much like cave-men living in dens of darkness, their understanding of Kingdom principles is dismal. Whereas many Christians are allured onto the poisonous path of prosperity and led astray. God wants to bless believers with something more meaningful than money. Seek spiritual gifts from God.

SEEDTIME

The Old Testament Actually Matters

It is very difficult, sometimes even impossible, to gain a clear understanding about spiritual principles using secular perspectives. God's thoughts are not our thoughts. Nevertheless, we must carefully examine the half-truths preached by self-righteous intellectuals, uneducated preachers, and inexperienced spiritualists. Manipulative myths must be dispelled to free the oppressed. Unfortunately, some of the most distinguished charismatic leaders falsely interpret scriptures. Some do so intentionally, others make mistakes and preach tradition. Coincidently, these false interpretations produce the same negative effects of oppression. They manipulate doctrines in order to serve their own selfish agendas and personal opinions. This is a monstrous evil. Some people use legal terminology to disqualify the OT. They poorly interpret the Bible using concepts that best suit modern-day law. They argue biblical perspectives using legal terms like Statute of Limitation and Double Jeopardy. They say the statute of limitation expired on the OT law when grace gave new meaning to NT believers. According to this anti-OT theology, God no longer has a moral standard for Christians. In their closing argument, they attempt to persuade believers that the OT is immaterial. Hence, holding Christians accountable to both the OT and NT is an inadmissible case of double jeopardy. They fail to realize that God is not limited to the NT. They fail to see beyond the shadows of God's wondrous works. Manmade changes cannot penetrate God's character. Notice the statue on the cover of this book referred to as Lady Justice. She has a sword in one hand and

140

the justice scale in the other. More importantly, she's blind-folded. These symbols are a fitting depiction of how God expects us to live life. Only God can produce the kind of change in our lives needed to stand the test of time. Times change, circumstances change, laws change and even people change, but God remains the same (see Hebrews 13:8). This means we must diligently search the scriptures to understand how God thinks. His principles are defined by his character. His character is outlined throughout the OT. The Holy Spirit is a gift that embodies believers specifically so that we can embody Christ. The only way for mankind to become one with God is through his word. The history and prophe-cies written in the OT give evidence that makes the NT more meaningful. Therefore, those who argue against the credibility of the OT are misguided. We should theologically deliberate until we understand God's motives. This means we must meditate on the entire Bible (see Psalms 1:2).

Study the Bible for Yourself

In order to best understand God's expectations about money matters, we must journey through the Bible. No one scripture is independent of the others. Different preachers misuse various Bible stories to support the new-aged pros-perity theology. For instance, they reference the woman who poured valuable oil on Jesus' feet. However, oil repre-sents anointing throughout the Bible, not money (see Leviti-cus 10:7, James 5:14). Oil is absolutely never used as a meta-phor for money. They also use the story about the poor widow who baked her last batch of bread for the prophet

Elijah. There again, we have another misrepresentation. Bread does not represent money nowhere throughout scripture. Jesus clearly taught us that bread represents the word of God. Cherry-picking scriptures to preach sermons for selfish gain is outright disgraceful. Additionally, people who fail to exegete the text are careless about the souls of their followers. According to the Apostle Paul, God's messages come by two or three witnesses (see I Corinthians 14:29). Likewise, every church doctrine or theology should be supported by multiple scriptures and different accounts. Additionally, God does not contradict himself and the Bible does not require personal interpretation. The three biblical concepts that are subject to interpretation are dreams, visions and tongues. Readers failing to study and poorly dividing the word of *Truth* simple miss the mark. To mathematically divide something is to systematically break it down into various portions. This means it is important to take one part of the Bible and measure its validity by using another part of it. This is an exegetical process (see Appendix A, Exegetical Process). An exegetical statement includes historical, grammatical, literary and contextual explanations. This exegetical process is a detailed analytical study of scripture. It enables readers to effectively answer one primary question, "What did the text originally mean?" Studying to discover the author's intent enlightens our understanding. It reveals the principles of God, unveils his secret thoughts, and illustrates his divine character. If we improperly exegete the text we dilute God's message, confuse listeners and pervert the *Truth*. The final step in any exegetical process should always include a concept called hermeneutics. This step turns an ancient Bible into an invaluable modern-day resource. It is also intended to answer one question, "How do the scriptures apply to us today?" Any other method of studying the Bible is considered reader-response. Responses based on personal experiences do not validate God's word. God wants to add evidence or substance to our hope. The Bible is the only credible source to balance doctrines. The truth prevails even without opinions and standing ovations. It does not matter what the scriptures mean to you. It only matters what the scriptures actually mean. Therefore, an exegetical approach is what we have used throughout this entire book.

Satan's Influence Controls Carnal Churches

In order for believers to understand the mysteries of the Bible, studying is a critical prerequisite. When Bible students find themselves confused after reading scriptures it is because the devil is trying to reconstruct your psyche into his playground. Satan is the best-selling author of confusion. The devil manipulates belief systems. He attempts to control, cultivate and captivate the way people think. Hence, people suffer the oppression of poverty—individuals lack critical resources necessary for spiritual development. Step outside the box? Forming the habit of reading takes time. Also, breaking poor study habits is even more difficult. Discipleship demands discipline. The devil consistently conceals, contaminates and changes his mix-message. Therefore, blindsided believers are deceived. They believe clichés that sound good. The truth will not always tickle your ear. The truth can actually hurt. God is not trying to harm us. Yet, the devil is. He aims at the targets of influential and powerful people. This is why apostles, prophets, evangelists, pastors and teachers must surrender to prayer and studying. Chasing prosperity and teaching others to do the same is a fatal distraction. The motto of every Christian leader must be, "Follow Christ." Instead, too many leaders encourage followers to follow in their own footsteps (see I Peter 2:21). Both non-believers and Christians who fail to study their own bibles carryout the devil's mission unknowingly. We are not expected to be Bible scholars, but God commands us to be Bible students—not just readers (see II Timothy 2:15). God rewards diligent seekers not casual readers (see Hebrews 11:6) Confident church leaders urge their members to set aside time to search the scriptures. Most Christians agree that studying the Bible is a basic expectation for believers. Instead of studying the Bible, some people only pretend. They claim to comprehend God's word, yet fail to even read it. This dishonest behavior is the back door into a worldwind of destructive deception. To this end, zealous Christians yearning for knowledge embrace drifting theories from television evangelists. They even embrace mythical opinions about money as Bible facts. They regurgitate rumors and accept anything that sounds logical as spiritual. They interject false images of themselves hoping to make others think they are spiritual-minded. Afterward, they unknowingly help spread half-truths throughout churches. Whereas the views and opinions of a once powerless devil ultimately controls many powerful churches. Under any other circumstance we'd call such people devil worshippers. Carefully examine yourself. *Seedtime* will repeatedly help you to see God's outlook on money matters, from Genesis to Revelation.

The First Biblical Reference of the Tithe

Defining what God expects concerning currency is a difficult subject. With no uncertainty, prosperity preachers have perverted the reputation of American churches. People are very private and passionate about their money—rightfully so. As a result of mismanaged church funds, many skeptics avoid church services all together. Instead of introducing lost souls to Jesus, many Christians have settled for the hope of new members. Likewise, prosperity leaders have an agenda to make as much money as possible. New members and more revenue are both beneficial, but God commands us to reconcile lost souls (see II Corinthians 5:18). For millenniums, finances and faith are two ingredients that clash like love and hate. About 70-percent of churchgoers say the tithe has nothing to do with their faith. Hence, less than 30-percent of most congregants tithe in America. Let's take an exegetical look at the tithe. Before the law was written, Abram gave a tithe to Melchizedek, the King of Salem. The King also served as the high priest of God. Melchizedek lived prior to the law and Levitical priesthood. Melchizedek means righteousness and Salem means peace. As well as, Melchizedek is the only known character in the OT that held both the titles of priest and king. According to Hebrews chapter 7, there is no record of his father, mother or descendants. There is neither trace of beginning of days, nor end of his life. Melchizedek's life resembles Christ. They are both high priests, symbols of righteousness, and ministers of peace. It is important to closely examine the first account of the tithe mentioned in the Bible. In order to best understand Abraham's actions, we must carefully consider his character, surroundings and experience.

The Life and Timeline of Abraham

This is the pattern of Abraham's life: In Genesis 11, his father Terah named his son Abram; In Genesis 12, God gives him a 6-fold promise. He said he would make him a great nation, bless him, make his name great, and cause him to be a blessing to others. God also promises to bless those who bless Abram and curse those who curse him; In Genesis 13, Abram and his nephew Lot were so rich that they deemed it best to live in separate places; In Genesis 14, four kings made war against five nations, to include the nation of Sodom, where Lot dwelled. When Abram heard that Lot was in captivity, he armed 318 trained servants, killed their enemies, rescued Lot, took possession of the goods, and set the captives free. Abram gave Melchizedek a tithe from the rewards they accumulated during the war. He gave the rest of the spoils to the King of Sodom. Abram's wealth had been previously established and he did not want anyone to take credit for making him rich. Hence, the tithe did not produce the wealth in Abraham's life. He was already rich. In Genesis 15, God speaks to Abram about the promise of an offspring, and refers to him as a seed, in the singular tense (see Galatians 3:16); In Genesis 16, When Abram was 86-years-old, his wife Sarai, influenced him to marry and have sex with her Egyptian handmaid Hagar. They produced a son, and named him Ishmael; In Genesis 17, God established the OT covenant between himself, Abram, and Abram's seed, which is Jesus Christ. God changed Abram's name to Abraham and Sarai's name to Sarah. As for Ishmael, God blessed him, made him fruitful, multiplied him exceedingly, caused him to produce 12 princes, and made him a great nation. God promises Abraham and Sarah that they'll produce a son and name him Isaac. He said that the covenant would descend through Isaac; In Genesis 18, three angels visit Abraham. Sarah laughs when she overhears the mentioning of a promise of a son, at her old age. Abraham pleads for the people of Sodom and Gomorrah; In Genesis 19, God rescues Abraham's nephew Lot from Sodom and Gomorrah; In Genesis 20, Abraham deceives King Abimelech into thinking that Sarah is his sister; In Genesis 21, Abraham is 100-years-old when Isaac was born. Hagar and Ishmael were sent away upon Sarah's request. Abraham and Abimelech made a treaty by the well at Beersheba; In Genesis 22, God tests Abraham's obedience, but provided a sacrifice in Isaac's stead; In Genesis 23, Abraham's wife, Sarah dies in Kirjatharba at age 127; In Genesis 24, Abraham grows old and prepares for his death; In Genesis 25, Abraham took another wife, Keturah. They conceived 6 children. He lived to be 195-years-old and then died. Ishmael and Isaac buried Abraham and Sarah in the cave of Machpelah, which means the double cave—God wants us to possess a double-portion of revelation.

Complacency vs. Contentment

There are three critical themes about Abraham's life as it relates to riches, the tithe, and his outlook on gaining more wealth. First, Abraham did not chase riches. He possessed wealth his entire life. His natural wealth was a result of a physical inheritance, hard work and wisdom. There was no lack in his life from birth to death. Abraham's life story is not centered on seeking selfish pleasures. On the contrary, his selfless sacrifices represented the kind of faith that pleases God. Secondly, Abraham's account of giving the tithe to Melchizedek was clearly an act of faith-filled gratitude. It is considered an act of gratitude because he demonstrated gratefulness for God's grace. During the brutal killings that took place to rescue Lot, Abraham's own life was spared through God's unmerited favor. This reality is made evident when Melchizedek appeared with bread and wine. Bread signifies the fact that Abraham's life was sustained. The wine represented cleansing from sins as a result of the bloodshed during the battle. Thirdly, it is considered an act of faith—he refused to benefit or prosper from the earthly possessions accumulated during the physical battle. Instead, Abraham expressed contentment with the riches he already possessed. The Apostle Paul says in the NT, godly contentment is great gain (see I Timothy 6:6). Modern-day prosperity seekers convince their followers that contentment is complacency. It is not. Contentment is exercising the discipline to be satisfied with what you have. Complacency is the misfortune of missing opportunities. God expects us to advance from one place in life to another. Abraham's life reflects a great journey of faith. He started by responding to God's initial instructions to leave his country and family. Abraham's character shows no signs of complacency. His godly contentment is defined by his discipline to deny added wealth. The scripture indicates that he did not want anyone to receive credit for making him rich (see Genesis 14:23). That's faith—reacting to the unseen—allowing God to present a powerful display of the invisible. He embraced a more meaningful purpose—one that actually matters to God. He'd already proved to possess the natural ability to acquire wealth on his own. Abraham was a man of immeasurable faith, humility and integrity. In all the wisdom of King Solomon, he identified money as the answer to all things (see Ecclesiastes 10:19). Abraham's lifelong outlook on money gives seekers the answers they need. He helps us to understand a powerful lessons about the tithe. Never expect riches as a spiritual reward for giving money. Never chase money—always chase what matters to God.

The Number Ten

Abraham's life lends believers a phenomenal testimony. The tithe is derived from a spiritual and powerful principle. The number 10 throughout the entire Bible has an underlined message, almost even secret, about responsibility, testimony and restoration. In fact, all numbers possess a spiritual significance. This is a mystery. For now, let's consider a few examples pertaining to the number ten. In Genesis chapter

149

1, we read 10 times, "God said." There were 10 generations before the flood. God gave Moses 10 commandments for the Israelites. Abraham concluded his prayer request for Sodom with 10 righteous people in the city. There were 10 plagues that came upon the people of Egypt and Pharaoh. There are 10 Psalms that begin with Hallelujah (see Psalms 106, 111, 112, 113, 135, 146, 147, 148, 149, and 150). Jesus tells the parable of 10 virgins. Jesus also tells the parable of the 10 servants and the 10 cities. The 8th chapter of Romans lists 10 oppositions that are unable to separate believers from God's love. The 6th chapter of Corinthians lists 10 vices that exclude people from the Kingdom of God. These ten examples are evidence of the spiritual principle associated with the number 10. Every account mentioned relating to the number 10 represents responsibility, testimony and restoration. Likewise, the tithe is a tenth. While the tithe is currently paid with currency, historically, agricultural products were used, i.e. herbs and fruit. Although the Mosaic law does not define our relationship with God, believers must accept some sort of financial responsibility. We are the benefactors of grace redeemed from the curse of the law. However, the OT tithe is a testimony that signifies to NT believers that we are still responsible for free-will giving. Greed, selfishness and ungratefulness causes people, preachers and entire churches to abandon the responsibility of giving to others.

An Unacceptable Tithe

Tithe means tenth, especially as offered to God. Abraham

gave a tithe to the priest-king of Jerusalem, Melchizedek (see Genesis 14:18-20). Jacob, who is also known as Israel, pledged to offer a tithe in response to God's favor (see Genesis 28:20-22). These two accounts took place prior to the law. Abraham and Jacob gave a tithe because of the grateful condition of their hearts. Israel's son Joseph brought his family to Egypt to protect them. After Joseph died, a new king arose in Egypt. The new Pharaoh did not know of Joseph. Whereas the children of Israel were forced into the most brutal form of slavery ever known in biblical history. The Bible makes no mention of the tithe while the people of God were under bitter bondage and oppression (see Exodus chapters 1-18). When God's people are suffering from oppression he calls leaders to liberate them. Whether it be socioeconomic, academic, physical or religious oppression, God expects leaders to make a change whenever and wherever injustices exists. *"He that oppresses the poor to increase his riches, and he that gives to the rich, shall surely come to want"* (Proverbs 22:16). This is a redundant theme for religious leaders (see Isaiah 61:1-3). Isaiah said it, and then Jesus echoed similar words. *"The Spirit of the Lord is upon me, because he has anointed me to preach the gospel to the poor; he has sent me to heal the broken hearted, to preach deliverance to the captives, and recovering of sight to the blind, to set at liberty them that are bruised. And to preach the acceptable year of Lord"* (Luke 4:18-19). It is totally unacceptable when leaders psychologically convince poor people that the tithe is a pre-requisite to receiving blessings from God. Instead of helping broken-hearted people break free from oppression, prosperity preachers poison

SEEDTIME

people in poverty and rob God. You might be wondering,
"How can a preacher rob God?" Whatever they do to the
least of those among us, Jesus says, they've done it as unto
him (see Matthew 25:45). It is an outright disgrace to human
dignity when preachers demand social-security disburse-
ments, monthly disability payments, welfare checks and
other forms of low-income in the name of the tithe and seed
offerings. These are struggling people with dire needs who
wouldn't otherwise survive without public assistance. The
Bible instructs believers to help such people, not to burden
them. Liberate the oppressed, do not pressure them for
money. Giving to gain social and spiritual acceptance is not
acceptable.

Worship Requires Worth

Upon conclusion of 400 years of slavery, God gave Moses
the 10 commandments, and additional laws to judge the Israelites (see Exodus 19—23). These commandments and
laws are important because they tell us how God expects us
to live. After the Great Exodus, known as the mass evacua-
tion from Egypt, the Israelites arrived safely at Mt. Sinai.
Upon arrival, God gave Moses instructions to build the first
tabernacle (see Exodus chapters 25-40). The tabernacle is a
place that enabled sinful people to maintain a relationship
with a Holy God. The book of Leviticus has 27 chapters
that outline what is expected as it relates to worshipping
God. It includes the following: 1. the burnt offering, 2. the
meat (grain) offering, 3. the peace offering, 4. the sin offering, 5. the trespass (guilt) offering, and 6. the memorial of-

fering. None of these offerings required money. Other responsibilities, including priestly duties are detailed in the book of Leviticus. God also set aside holy holidays such as 1. the Passover and festival of unleavened bread, 2. the festival of fruits, 3. the festival of Pentecost, 4. the day of atonement, 5. the festival of tabernacles, and 6. the year of Jubilee. The book of Leviticus concludes after 27 chapters. The timeline is 500-years after the previous reference of the tithe. Remember, the commandments and laws taught the Israelites how to live, and the offerings and holy days taught them the value of worship. Unfortunately, they failed to recognize the spiritual significance of these feast days. Likewise, modern-day Christians fail to recognize the same. If you want your worship to possess worth learn to value what God does. What do these offerings and holidays mean to you?

Most Misunderstood Message about Money

The Israelites continuously failed to obey the Mosaic Law and dishonored the covenant of their forefather Abraham. As a result, God established a new covenant through Jesus Christ, Abraham's promised seed. Jesus was born through an immaculate conception as the Savior of the world. He came to re-establish relationship between God and mankind. He lived on earth for 33-years. As the son of God, he demonstrates and illustrates the ultimate example for Christians to follow. Through his brutal death he redeemed followers from the curse of the law. He also reconciled believers from sin. Jesus permanently fulfilled the mandatory requirements of the law. However, it is important to note that some stipulations written in Leviticus were guidelines for voluntary worship. God gives freewill; believers must make a choice to live a lifestyle of worship or chase after wealth (se Luke 16:33). Even though Christ fulfilled the mandatory requirements of the law, he did not destroy it. True believers possess a deep desire to voluntarily surrender to God. The law characterizes the way God thinks. Christ is the perfect portrayal of God's thoughts. God's expectations are not secret. Cain's meaningless offering and Abel's meaningful sacrifice reveals God's thoughts about spiritual sacrifices vs. physical possessions. Unfortunately, most people error in the way of Cain. *"Woe unto them! For they have gone in the way of Cain, and ran greedily after the error of Balaam for reward, and perished in the gainsaying of Core"* (Jude 1:11). Core is the Greek spelling of the Hebrew name Korah, who is the grandson of Esau. They represent a family lineage of Edomites who trade spiritual promises for physical possession. Money can never buy or even bolster the gifts of God (see Acts 8:20). The selfless sacrifice of surrendering praise and worship is the kind of priceless worth God expects. In essence, there is absolutely no monetary substance that can replace true worship. All the physical provisions on this planet could not purchase intimacy with God. Those who attempt to access spiritual gifts or blessings with dollar bills will perish with their money.

Illusions Intended to Entice

We are spiritual-beings. Our bodies will eventually decay, and our possessions will ultimately be destroyed along with

154

the earth. Money is just an illusion, and so are other physical aspects of life. They enable individuals to measure the condition of their hearts. What you do with currency will tell you a lot about your character. This must remain a redundant theme in order to prisoners of prosperity to break free. Remember, wherever your treasure is there shall your heart be (see Matthew 6:21). This is why Jesus warns us not to store our treasures in this world. A treasure is what people consider to be their most valuable asset. Some people value material things, like cash, cars and clothes. Other people treasure spiritual things, like love, joy, peace, patience, kindness, goodness, faithfulness, gentleness and self-control (see Galatians 5:22-23). There is one distinct difference between an illusion and reality. Realities are incorruptible, indisputable and incomprehensible. Illusions are based on mere mental perceptions. Most people remain trapped in a world of illusions throughout their entire lives. When wealth becomes your priority materialism will play tricks on your mind. Prosperity spectators will always find themselves desperately wanting more. A far greater destiny awaits people who are no longer enticed by illusions. Only a visit with the heavenly physician will enable sin sick souls to consume a dose of reality. Realities are extensions of God, but illusions will fade away. During the Gulf War, I fought in Kuwait and Iraq nearly 6 months with C Company 2/16th Infantry Battalion. The United States Department of Defense classified the conflict as Desert Storm. I served our country in the same platoon with the Oklahoma bomber, Timothy McVeigh. Despite his cruel and unusual display of dishonor, he was no different from any other delusional person. He possessed twisted mental perceptions. Only in his case, illusions resulted in the natural death of innocent civilians—men, women and children. Illusions of physical prosperity also destroys desperate people. During Desert Storm, some soldiers unnecessarily risked their lives while fighting on the frontlines. Extremely hot middle-eastern temperatures of more 100 degrees, dry heat and limited water supplies created delusional affects. During mid-day battles, dehydrated and desperately thirsty soldiers chased after pools of water that actually did not exist. These day-visions are called mirages. They are nothing more than optical illusions based on deep desires. Civilians have illusions also. Their illusions are based on wealth, relationships and power. Everyone battles with illusions created by their own egos and emotions. Christians must make sure not to chase wells of wealth and prosperity waterfalls that actually do not exist. People who chase money lose sight of the things that actually matter. What matters most is seeing the world through the Creator's perspective. In order to do so, we must walk by faith. We must embrace God as our only true reality, and allow our inner-spirit to become one with him. Jesus said, *"Let them that worship, worship in spirit and in truth"* (John 4:24). According to the Mosaic Law, worship requires worth. This is why the devil tries to influence people to connect with material things that have no spiritual value. When Satan is successful, believers become disconnected. Praise and worship allows us to experience intimacy with God, but illusions are intended to entice.

Slavery Starts and Ends in the Mind

Despite the new covenant established with Christ's blood, some people are stuck in the same thought-patterns. Instead of studying the Bible, many people are controlled by pulpit officials. Freedom has a lot to do with the way the mind processes knowledge. This is why so countless religious victims are enslaved and most don't even know it. My deceased grandparents were sharecroppers in the Mississippi Delta. As descendants of slaves, they were uneducated concerning their civil rights. In 1970, I was born, over 100 years after the 1863 Emancipation Proclamation. Yet, we lived in an original slave shack relocated from a nearby plantation. During the Spring of 2008, Ambassador Academy staff member, Cassandra Moody and myself took an urban group of 9th graders on a mission trip to Mississippi. The wooden structure still stands in a small town called Lambert. During the tour, students took pictures. They reacted as if they were a part of some distant historical experience. In reality, the same type of oppression is alive and well today. Prior to the Civil War, the state of Mississippi made more millionaires per capita than any other state in the union. Cotton was the crop that made sharecropping abundantly lucrative. The plantation owners misused and manipulated my family for cheap labor. As a result, they gained filthy lucre. Despite the unfairness, my grandfather, Johnny Ellis Thigpen Sr., who we affectionately called Big-Daddy, understood what matters most. Big-Daddy's happiness had nothing to do with financial prosperity. Despite our physical lack, we were never in poverty. In reality we were rich in righteousness, love, joy and forgiveness. My grandparents even named one of their eight children after the plantation owner. I'm told that Bid-Daddy worked long-hard days. He possessed a reputation as the Christian who never complained. Most of what I remember about Big-Daddy has been passed down through generations. Here's what I personally recall. The world felt like a better place whenever he was around. A part of me will always feel like he deserved so much more. However, I'm confident that wealth would not have made a difference with his beliefs. The wealthy plantation owner had many possessions, but he did not possess integrity like Big-Daddy. Big-Daddy loved and treated everybody right. The plantation owner misused sharecroppers for cheap labor. Sometimes it's hard to believe Big-Daddy was just a mortal man. Big-Daddy's spirit was bigger than words can describe. Like so many other phenomenal people that we seldom read about, Big-Daddy died with the dignity of a hero. Until death, he happily lived in the same shotgun-style-slave shack. He did not escape the aftermath of slavery. He did not combat the injustice imposed by segregation. He did not get revenge on his oppressor. However, his integrity makes me proud to be a Thigpen. Countless Christians are still enslaved today. They fail to escape the bondage of hatred, racism and unforgiveness. Slavery starts in the mind. People who focus on physical experiences continuously suffer spiritual consequences (see Philippians 2:3, 5). Don't allow the devil to hypnotize you into hating what actually matters to God and wanting more of worldly wealth.

Tracing the History of the Tithe

History is essential to our destiny. Family, world and religious history enables people to avoid repeat mistakes. After making mention of the Mosaic Law, the tithe is only supported 4 times in biblical history. Each account is in the OT (see Numbers 18:21, II Chronicles 31:5-6, Nehemiah 3:12, Malachi 3:8). The tithe is not re-implemented within the NT. Although the OT explains the tithe, it is not a known practice in the NT. For more than 700-years after the NT Church was established, the tithe was completely ignored. The Catholic Church is known to be the oldest existing entity of organized Christian religion. Their records indicate that the tithe was not adopted for over seven centuries after the crucifixion of Christ. Although initially rejected in councils at Tours in 567 AD and Macon in 585 AD, Pope Adrian I formally recognized the tithe in 787 AD. Since then, the tithe has become a routine practice. It is frequently preached from the pulpit in most churches. Different denominations continue to view the tithe differently. In recent years, the tithe is taught as a form of stewardship God requires. The prosperity theology is more complicated as it relates to the tithe. Such leaders teach that God will physically bless those who give and physically curse those who do not. The primary basis to this argument is that God has never formally abolished the tithe. When rumors circulated throughout the early church about the law, Paul dispelled the lies (see Acts 15:24-29). He warned believers to avoid unnecessary burdens. When church leaders create rules and consequences centered on contributions they misrepresent Christ.

SEEDTIME

Self-Serving Doctrines and the Early Church

Some NT writers do occasionally mention church finances. However, they never make an appeal supporting the tithe. This approach continued for several centuries. Cyprian is a Catholic leader who wondered whether the tithe should be re-introduced. Although it did not happen during his lifetime, he aimed to re-implement elements of the OT Levitical system. He stated concerns that ministry leaders were not always receiving deserved respect. He expressed interest in exalting ministry leaders above members of the congregation. He maintained two primary concerns. First, he warned against schism, which is division and splits within the church. Secondly, he warned against heretics, which are congregants who do not conform to the doctrines as defined by church leaders. The Apostle Paul was considered a heretic by the leaders of the Jewish church. *"For we have found this man a pestilent fellow, and a mover of sedition among all the Jews throughout the world, and a ringleader of the sect of the Nazarenes: Who also hath gone about to profane the temple"* (Acts 24:5-6). Paul was a ringleader amongst the Nazarenes who spoke up against false teachings. As stated previously, Nazarenes are people who make vows and expect nothing in return. Paul purposed to keep God's people pure from physical lusts, despite personal persecution. When most leaders feel threatened they falsely accuse those who speak against their false doctrines. Cyprian's solution for such concerns was to place ministry leaders on a pedestal. When authoritarians stand over people and give instructions it indirectly effects the esteem of the listener. By raising the pulpit higher parishioners

160

were forced to look up. Psychologically this made leaders feel more important and gain recognition and added respect. In turn, it made parishioners feel like they were not equal to those who stood center mass on high pedestals. The word pulpit is referenced one time in the entire Bible (see Nehemiah 8:4). A pulpit is described as an elevated platform without a lectern, high reading desk, or podium. According to the book of Nehemiah, Ezra built a pulpit to preach one sermon during difficult times. He did so for one reason. He felt the need to give solidity and strength to the Jewish community struggling against pressures to surrender its theological identity. He used the pulpit to excerpt authority. Centuries later, Catholic officials did so to advance their own selfish agendas. Modern-day clergy have no idea how evil influences crept into the church. Whereas people with no knowledge of these historical hindrances are prone to repeat the same mistakes. Many ritualistic aspects of religion can be traced back to Cyprian's influence within the Catholic church.

Inappropriate Use of Authority

Constantine ruled as the first Christian emperor. Many historians suspect that he was never actually converted to Christianity. For this reason, serious thought and great debates thrived about church finances. Soon after, ministry leaders claimed to construct magnificent buildings in honor of Christ. When in fact, they exalted men more than the Master. Congregants soon realized that these leaders actually built monuments to themselves. Finances became an even

161

greater issue. Larger facilities cost more money. Having a Christian emperor caused Christianity to become respectable throughout society. The majority of martyrs and Christian persecution ceased. The influence of the Christian emperor caused many people, even some who had not been converted, to pour financial resources into the visible church. As previously stated, when Christianity became the primary influence of a domain, the term Christendom prevailed. Leadership often fell into the hands of bishops. History records that these bishops were really politicians—they were much more secular than they were men of God. This organized system of government led to the politically imposed tithe. A system despised by many because it was forcefully imposed. Yet, perhaps nothing has made the established church more hated than the abuse of this misappropriated taxation. Churches that teach the concept of the tithe—in our day— seem genuinely unaware of this hideous system. Many modern-day Christians are unaware that various countries forced citizens to pay the tithe as a tax. In fact, it wasn't abolished in England and Wales until the Tithe Act of 1936, less than 75-years-ago.

Prosperity Preachers Apply Pressure

In many countries, the tithe was linked to the tax system. Tax payers were religiously oppressed with taxation without representation for over 1,000 years. The Catholic Church accessed the government funds. Whereas Catholicism remains the wealthiest Christian religion in the world. Catholic officials did not preach prosperity to gain wealth. However, they disguised elected and appointed officials as Christians. Likewise, they disguised the countless disgraceful acts of child molestation in recent years. The Catholic Church continues to reap economic and political benefits under various disguises. In 1936, Public-Law put an end to forcing people to pay charitable contribution in the form of taxes. By then, religious leaders discovered many other means of making money. Furthermore, more than 100-years-ago, history exposed how the Catholic Church reaped financial increase from the African Slave Trade. Slavery ended as an indirect result of the Emancipation Proclamation sign by President Abraham Lincoln. Although, Lincoln's ambitions had little to do with the liberation of African slaves. He stumbled upon the issue of slavery while trying to salvage power for the position of presidency. Southern states like South Carolina, Mississippi, Florida, Alabama, Georgia, Louisiana and Texas removed themselves from the union prior to his presidency. Lincoln, a resident of Illinois, was believed to be anti-slavery. The Civil War actually took place because the southern agriculturalists and northern industrialist possessed opposing economic views. When southern states wanted to prevent the control of federal government the north and south were divided. Hence, we experienced the Civil War. To this end, slavery was abolished. However, many Catholics and Protestants in the south were made multi-millionaires as a result of slave labor and sharecropping. Money makes many religious leaders, politicians and everyday individuals ruin the lives of others for personal gain. We must stay focused on Christ in order to liberate the oppressed. Similar injustices continue today. As a result of the Constitutional separation between Church and State, government ignores religious oppression. In the name of freedom of religion, oppression thrives, cults survive, and the misuse of charitable contributions are validated through federal tax exemptions. Something has to be done. Church members who do not pay the tithe are forced to feel guilty. Even worse, churchgoers are criticized and counted as cursed if they do not give. This effects how poverty takes on new dimensions—high hopes of financial prosperity influence suffering communities. Citizens transform into criminals in order to take possession of what prosperity preachers purport. The prosperity message causes a perverse effect on people in impoverished communities. Community churches used to play a significant role defining moral standards. The new-aged prosperity theology causes people to focus on money and materialism. Whereas the masses set their affections on earthly possessions. Various communities no longer possess spiritual values. Confused Christians hustle to fulfill high hopes of physical prosperity. Considering that the love of money is the root of all evil, urban communities are suffering from immorality. In part, the prosperity theology is to blame, and those who purport it are guilty. Prosperity preachers bolster financial blessings for those who give. They often think their churches will belly-flop financially if they do not manipulate their members. This is far from the truth. People give to good causes. Do not surrender to Satan pressure that causes oppression. Study the Bible and learn to treasure the truth.

Chapter **7**

The Perfect Crime

Prosperity Churches Competing With Casinos

Prosperity churches and casinos have a lot in common *"For many walk, of whom I have told you often, and now tell you even weeping, that they are the enemies of the cross of Christ: Whose end is destruction, whose God is their belly, and whose glory is in their shame, who mind earthly things"* (Philippians 3:19). Do not gamble away your soul trying to fulfill fantasies of physical possessions. Consider how most modern-day casinos across America operate. They are located in areas suffering from limited resources, high unemployment rates, and poorly performing schools. The primary marketing strategy of modern-day casinos is basic textbook marketing—create an illusion, and then appeal to the need. They build in places like Gary and East Chicago Indiana, Tunica and Vicksburg Mississippi, New Orleans, Louisiana, Pittsburg, Pennsylvania, Detroit, Michigan and Milwaukee, Wisconsin. The demographics define areas that are densely populated with needy people. Odds have it that people in impoverished areas are willing to risk what they have. They gamble social security checks, welfare assistance, disability allowances, pensions and even death benefits. Very few people win big. Casinos are strategically designed to strip the masses of everything they have. The lavish and luxurious architectural structures are alluring. However, the communities they colonize suffer significantly. They do provide jobs, but they ultimately help ruin the moral fabric of urban America. Wealthy individuals without economic limitations gamble for different motives. To them, losing a bet is nothing more than entertainment in the Gaming Industry.   However, desperate gamblers risk everything they trade deeds to their houses and entire paychecks. By its nature, losers commit suicide, suffer depression and divorce. Casinos and prosperity churches both have special seating reserved for big spenders and VIP guests. Prosperity churches and casinos capitalize and prey on hopeful people. They both advertise false hopes. They conveniently accept multiple methods of payment—ATM machines are readily available. Wherever marketers make merchandise available money is usually accessible. Simply stated, prosperity churches and casinos are lucrative business markets. Perhaps Donald Trump, Don Barden and Steve Wynn should have gone to seminary schools. If so, as preachers, they could receive tax exemptions. They could also hire inspirational and motivational speakers and call their casinos churches. In turn, they would gain constitutional protection through the Separation of Church and State. Unfortunately, most prosperity preachers don't even understand the Bible. Even self-taught religious leaders are able to identify the difference between physical possessions and spiritual promises. When churches compete against casinos nobody wins.

The Storehouse is not the Church

Storehouses were built to prevent pointless community loses of harvested crops. There is a distinct difference between storehouses and churches. Storehouses were built as storages throughout Israel. They were used to protect herbs and fruit from extreme weather conditions. Storehouses were rectangular structures divided into three narrow aisles. Israeli tabernacles were often made of tents and transported throughout the middle-east. Throughout history storehouses were solid structures that were specifically designed to remain stationary. Large-thick walls supported the roof. Made of stones weighing 400 pounds, the walls were 11-feet high. The etymology of the word temple has a prefix of temp, as in temporary or constantly changing. The NT suggests that our bodies are God's temples (see I Corinthians 3:6). The compound etymology of the word storehouse has a two-fold meaning. A Store is a place were supplies are consistently kept. A house is a permanent place of residence. *"Therefore, my beloved brethren, be ye steadfast, unmovable, always abounding in the work of the Lord, forasmuch as ye know that your labor is not in vain in the Lord"* (I Corinthians 15:58). Community storehouses were specifically used as public markets. Middle-eastern nations possessed great wealth, but storehouses were never shelters for money. During one period in Israeli history, royal storehouses were established in regional capitals to collect tax payments. During this era of taxation, taxes were only paid with flour, oil, grain or wine, despite the existence of a common currency. Likewise, communion consists of bread and wine. Flour and grain are both symbolic of the word of God—not money. Oil and wine are figurative images of power—not money. Therefore, even when mandatory taxes were collected in storehouses the significance had nothing to do with money. Storehouses were often built near temples, sometimes they were even connected. Whereas, utensils for worship and other religious valuables were located therein. Storehouses are similar to safety deposit boxes, but unlike traditional bank accounts.

Storehouses were never used as storages for money. Prophets used storehouses as a spiritual setting to minister to God. However, Priest used temples as a temporal location to minister to people. Storehouses are quite different from temples. Storehouses are figurative of the human spirit. Temples are comparable to church facilities. *"Howbeit the most High dwelleth not in temples made with hands; as saith the prophet"* (Acts 7:48). Modern-day religious leaders place stronger emphasis on church attendance, instead of daily lifestyles. God desires communion with Christians. *"God is a Spirit: and they that worship him must worship him in spirit and in truth"* (John 4:24). Storehouses and temples are both significant. Believers must seek to define the difference between spiritual and physical principles. Afterward, we must put religious practices in the right perspective.

Prophets Protect and Preserve God's Word

A prophet is one who speaks the word of God. *"For when for the time ye ought to be teachers, ye have need that one teach you again which be the first principles of the oracles of God; and are become such as have need of milk, and not of strong meat"* (Hebrews 5:12). Meat is used throughout the Bible as a figurative depiction of God's word (see Genesis 1:26, I Corinthians 3:2, Matthew 25:42, John 4:8, 32, 34, John 6:27, I Corinthians 10:3, Hebrews 5:12, 14, Malachi 1:12, 3:10). The OT is completely based on types and shadows (see Hebrews 10:1). Everything pertaining to the storehouse had a spiritual significance. 1. The three aisles represent the sovereignty of the Godhead. 2. The flour, oil, grain and wine represent the power of

God's written word. 3. The harvested crops represent God's spoken word. 4. The valuable assets represent our worth to God. 5. The utensils of worship represent God's worth to us. 6. The presence of the prophets signifies that the storehouse was a currency exchange. It is a place where we dedicate ourselves to God. Ultimately, the storehouse is a place of continued worship. The storehouse is figurative of anywhere you decide to commune with God. God has given us the gift of his Spirit, which enables us to understand his word. Hence, spirit-filled believers should protect and preserve the authentic meaning of the Bible.

Meat has Nothing to do with Money

The OT is all too often misunderstood. Therefore, many church doctrines are assembled based on assumptions. *"Bring ye all the tithes into the storehouse, that there may be meat in mine house, and prove me now herewith, says the Lord of hosts, if I will not open you the windows of heaven, and pour you out a blessing, that there shall not be room enough to receive it"* (Malachi 3:10). Mere assumptions cause modern-day Christians to identify the storehouse as the visible church. Mere assumptions also cause church members to think meat is a metaphor for money. Remember, storehouses are not temples and meat is not money. Furthermore, do not manipulate the biblical definition of meat to make money. *"God said, Behold, I have given you every herb bearing seed, which is upon the face of all the earth, and every tree, in the which is the fruit of a tree yielding seed; to you it shall be for meat"* (Genesis 1:29). God identifies the seed of herb and the seed of fruit as meat. *"Now the parable is this: The seed is the word of God"* (Luke 8:11). God blesses us with two measures of spiritual seed. Spirit-filled believers who study the Bible possession a double-portion of God's power (see I Kings 18:32). We read the written word, which is called Logos in the Greek vernacular. We are also supposed to hear the spoken word, which Greeks call Rhema. Without Logos, the Rhema has no foundational support. Without Rhema, the Logos cannot be properly understood. Herb and fruit work hand-in-hand (see Genesis 1:29). Unfortunately, everybody cannot handle meat. By its nature, every Christian, despite their church title, cannot handle this book. *"But strong meat belongeth to them that are of full age, even those who by reason of use have their senses exercised to discern both good and evil"* (Hebrews 5:14). The KJV Bible uses the word meat 275 times. Meat has the same spiritual connotation from Genesis to Revelation. *"Moreover, brethren, I would not that ye should be ignorant, how that all our fathers were under the cloud, and all passed through the sea; And were all baptized unto Moses in the cloud and in the sea; And did all eat the same spiritual meat"* (I Corinthians 10:1-3). God's intentions do not changed. He expects meat in the storehouse and money is no substitute.

Two Kinds of Seed Are Required to Tithe

The mysterious tithe requires both seed of herb and fruit. Herbs are naturally grown supplement used for a variety of purposes. Herbal plant-life is used to extract a botanical agent that creates dye. Herbs are used to create multiple fragrances and perfumes. Some herbs possess cleansing agents and natural healing capabilities. Herbs also add seasoning to food and have a host of other benefits. Jesus said, *"But woe unto you, Pharisees! For ye tithe mint and rue and all manner of herbs, and pass over judgment and the love of God: these ought ye to have done, and not to leave the other undone"* (Luke 11:42). The Pharisees were guilty. They only brought the portion of the tithe to the storehouse that satisfied their own selfish desires. Preachers who are money manipulators turn a blind eye to scriptural text that expose their own sinful tactics. *"Ye blind guides, which strain at a gnat, and swallow a camel. Woe unto you, scribes and Pharisees, hypocrites! for ye make clean the outside of the cup and of the platter, but within they are full of extortion and excess"* (Matthew 23-24-25). Extortion is defined as the crime of obtaining money or some other thing of value by the abuse of one's office or authority. Dictionary sources state that extortion is oppressive by nature. Pharisees gave the herb and ignored the fruit. The herb is for healing, beautification, cleansing, enhancing and edifying. *"But the fruit of the Spirit is love, joy, peace, longsuffering, gentleness, goodness, faith, Meekness, temperance: against such there is no law"* (Galatians 5:22-23). Make sure you have fruit in your storehouse—stock spiritual resources in the secret chambers of your soul. Now that we understand the storehouse is not the sanctuary, meat is not money, and seed is not currency, stop confusing spiritual blessings with physical possessions.

Physical Shadows of Spiritual Things

As sub-titled previously, *Something Everybody Needs to Know about the Number Ten,* (see: Reader Focus Writing Index) God holds us responsible for our lifestyles. As a reminder, there are 10 commandments, 10 plagues of Egypt, the parable of the 10 virgins and many more. Every single Bible story, which mentions the number 10 has everything to do with responsibility, testimony and restoration. The tithe was intended to help three groups of people. A Levitical tithe helped supply agricultural resources to priests (see Numbers 18:20-32). Now, under the covenant of Christ, NT believers are considered God's royal priesthood (see I Peter 2:9). Therefore, there should be meat in our individual lives. The second tithe was used to host a family feast in the sanctuary celebrating the harvest. They also celebrated with agricultural resources (see Deuteronomy 14:22-27). The third mentioning of tithe was to care for the widows, orphans, non-Israeli nations and the priest. Again, money never served as a substitute resource for agricultural products (see Deuteronomy 14:28-29). The OT description of the tithe is difficult to comprehend without the NT revelation from Christ. The physical duties sometimes overshadow the spiritual significance of the law. Students and clergy must search the scriptures diligently.

Stop Chasing Shadows

The Bible is clear concerning God's warning about the end times. *"This know also, that in the last days perilous times shall come. For men shall be lovers of their own selves, covetous, boasters, proud, blasphemers, disobedient to parents, unthankful, unholy, Without natural affection, trucebreakers, false accusers, incontinent, fierce, despisers of those that are good, Traitors, heady, high-minded, lovers of pleasures more than lovers of God; Having a form of godliness, but denying the power thereof: from such turn away"* (II Timothy 3:1-5). Turn away from leaders who teach you to focus on earthly promises, physical possessions and prideful egos—you've been warned. Prosperity seekers fail to embrace the significance of suffering. *"That I may know him, and the power of his resurrection, and the fellowship of his sufferings, being made conformable unto his death"* (Philippians 3:10). God expects us to experience longsuffering in order to develop Christian character (see I Peter 4:1, 5:10, II Timothy 1:12, 2:12). Perhaps you thought God does not expect us to endure heartache. *"These things I have spoken unto you, that in me ye might have peace. In the world ye shall have tribulation: but be of good cheer; I have overcome the world"* (John 16:33). Leaders who try to navigate their flock to avoid tribulation and suffering fail to preach the power of the cross (see I Corinthians 1:18). Tribulation should not tamper with your joy. People who rely on money more than God miss the mark and forsake spiritual gladness (see Proverbs 10:28). Money will fail. The current recession is proof of this reality. Prosperity bitten Christians claim that they do not suffer from recession. However, when the American dollar loses its value, everybody suffers—the rich and poor alike. A recession is a reduction in a country's gross domestic product. Even God's chosen people suffered a recession during the days of Israel. Hence, they went to Egypt for help. Much like America is relying on the support of China during its 2009 economic recession. God assures us throughout the Bible that money is not a reliable resource. *"And when money failed in the land of Egypt, and in the land of Canaan, all the Egyptians came unto Joseph, and said, Give*

174

us bread: for why should we die in thy presence? for the money fails" (Genesis 47:15). It is certain that one day money will permanently lose its value, based on the Bible. *"And that no man might buy or sell, save he that had the mark, or the name of the beast, or the number of his name"* (Revelation 13:17). People who rely on worldly resources as their ultimate source are marked by Satan's persuasion. We must allow faith in God's word to consume our Christian walk—not even this book. It is important for every believer to see life from God's perspective. Our intent is to cast down the shadows and images and refocus Christianity on Christ.

Why Animals Were Sacrificed

Money-hounds are spiritual-vipers. They deceive themselves and others. These seeing eye dogs lead blind followers to an eternal pit. *"Beware of dogs, beware of evil workers, beware of the concision. For we are the circumcision, which worship God in the spirit, and rejoice in Christ Jesus, and have no confidence in the flesh"* (Philippians 3:2-3). God wants us to see spiritual things. Otherwise Satan will catch us with his cunning traps. *"Let them alone: they be blind leaders of the blind. And if the blind lead the blind, both shall fall into the ditch"* (Matthew 15:14). The closest living thing in creation to man is an animal. We were made on the same day, taken from the same earth, and both possess life. The only thing that gives our lives more meaning than animal-life is that God breathed into man. *"And the Lord God formed man of the dust of the ground, and breathed into his nostrils the breath of life; and man became a living soul"* (Genesis 2:7). God transformed us from physical to spiritual-beings.

Man became something out of the ordinary. Before the sinful fall of mankind we possessed spiritual dominion. Modern-day prosperity leaders confuse our spiritual dominion with earthly authority. Upon death, our physical bodies will be eaten by maggots. God's intent is to reconcile our living souls back into his eternal presence. Animals on the other hand, will return to the earth. *"Who knows the spirit of man that goes upward, and the spirit of the beast that goes downward to the earth"* (Ecclesiastes 3:21)? God instructed us to make animal sacrifices because it is a form of spiritual worship. Animals have spirits although they have no souls. For this reason, dogs focus on physical bones and believers supposedly seek spiritual integrity. God wants praise and worship (see John 4:24, I Peter 2:9). However, he does not egotistically want us to exalt him. Instead, worship represents our intimate connection to God and praise provides him with a habitation in our soul. The concept of animal sacrifices suggests the importance of a spiritual atonement. Unfortunately, prosperity leaders fail to focus on faith. They do not protect the flock from lustful desires like good shepherds should (see Jeremiah 50:6, Ezekiel 44:10, Matthew 18:12, II Peter 2:15). Therefore, many sheep are gone astray.

Desperate for Dollars

Some people, even some church leaders, have been set free from the deception of financial prosperity. However, compromising leaders neglect to re-program their misguided members. After God exposes us to the truth we have a responsibility to liberate others (see Isaiah 1:17). Instead of teaching the truth, many leaders allow their supporters to walk in darkness. The so-called prosperity gospel defines seed as money, the tithe as money, and meat as money— money, money, and more money. They are unequivocally desperate for dollars. The issue of the tithe is seldom mentioned in the NT. Jesus introduced believers to the reality of being born again—as in, born of the spirit. It's very clear that Jesus wants us to understand the importance of the tithe and offerings from a spiritual perspective (see John 6:63). He focuses on what they spiritually represent, as opposed to physical requirements. Likewise, his disciples taught churches to give cheerfully, not grudgingly. Most importantly we should give from the heart (see II Corinthians 9:7). The Apostle Paul, who wrote more books of the NT than any other writer, never instructed churches to tithe. Cheerful giving continued for centuries, until church leaders became even more desperate for dollars. According to the early Apostles, mandatory giving is not God's intention. Born again believers are free from the law. However, when leaders become desperate for dollars oppression is a guaranteed side-affect.

How the Tithe Resurfaced

The tithe resurfaced amongst believers when Christendom grew. Considering this, its' majority influence populated various domains. Bishops were the known leaders of these dominions. Bishops were political leaders who also ruled in Christian communities. They served as bishops merely for political influence. In areas populated with a Christian ma-

177

jorities, they gained votes. Pay-for-Play politics was a common practice amongst political leaders in the world of religion. The word Catholic means universal. Catholism is the earliest known denomination in Christianity. Other denomination are said to have descended from the universal church. Catholics connect their denominational experience to biblical references about the Apostle Peter. He is recorded as the first official bishop of the universal church. By 787 AD, civil law made the tithe an obligation to citizens in the Carolingian empire. By the tenth century, the tithe was a civil law in England, Whales and several other countries. Much history has been written about the anger and hatred these civil laws imposed in England and Germany. Oftentimes, corrupt bishops, similar to prosperity leaders today, publicly lived lavish and luxurious lifestyles. Without any regard to those who lived in lack, these bishops flaunted the proceeds collected by people who were struggling to survive. This is a precise depiction of religious oppression today. These bishops facilitated the purchases of land and properties. The Catholic church benefited from untold wealth by means of this strategic system of financial prosperity. It was not until recent years that the Tithe Act of 1936, put a stop to this taxation. The tithe by taxation gained the support of government to advance the Catholic church. The tithe is enforced by the fear of being cursed in modern-day churches. Even still, some people tithe based on religious tradition, and others do so voluntarily. However, most Christians fail to study the historical significance of the tithe.

Chapter **8**

Eternal Desire

SEEDTIME

Eternal Desire

One moment with God will transform temporal ambitions into eternal desires. *"One thing have I desired of the Lord, that will I seek after; that I may dwell in the house of the Lord all the days of my life, to behold the beauty of the Lord, and to inquire in his temple"* (Psalms 27:4). Most people ignore invisible things. "Out of sight, out of mind," is a common cliché amongst the masses. Christians must realize that we are more spiritual than we are physical. Our bodies will soon perish, but our souls will live forever. *"For what shall it profit a man, if he shall gain the whole world, and lose his own soul"* (Mark 8:36)? Jesus told Martha that one thing is needful (see Luke 10:42). Most people have multiple goals and personal ambitions. Only one thing is truly important to believers wanting to please God. *"Brethren, I count not myself to have apprehended: but this one thing I do, forgetting those things which are behind, and reaching forth unto those things which are before"* (Philippians 3:13). Perhaps we should rethink our ambitions. The Bible indicates what we should think about and what not to think about. Take no thought for your life. Take no thought for food and clothes. Take no thought for tomorrow. Take no thought for what you shall say (see Matthew 6:25-34, Mark 13:11). On the flip side, the Bible also instructs us what to think about. Think on things that are true, honest, just, pure, lovely, and a good report (see Philippians 4:8). *"The desire of the righteous is only good: but the expectation of the wicked is wrath"* (Proverbs 11:23). God wants us to focus our desires on things above, instead of living life based on physical expectations.

Addictions Make People Lie to Themselves

Believers who ask for physical prosperity are like pagan worshippers. They want, request and desire physical pleasures more than spiritual promises. People who are addicted to physical pleasures enjoy the conveniences and fail to face reality. In theory, a pathological liar is no different from a habitual shopper. They are both controlled by carnal desires rather than being led by the Spirit of God. Habitual liars and "shopalohics" both suffer similar consequences. They fail to change reality and waste years trying. It is impossible to worship both God and money (see Matthew 2:24). This is why some people will die in pursuit of happiness. *"For they that are after the flesh do mind the things of the flesh; but they that are after the Spirit the things of the Spirit. For to be carnally minded is death; but to be spiritually minded is life and peace. Because the carnal mind is enmity (hatred) against God"* (Romans 8:5-7). People who get mixed up in materialism have convinced themselves that God actually cares about temporal things. This chapter will help believers seek the things that actually matter to God.

Worship Without Physical Expectations

Prosperity churches are blood thirsty vampires. They want the power of God, but not his presence. Such churches are time conscience. They place time restraints on praise and worship. By its nature, more services per Sunday generate more wealth. People are pushed through like grazing cattle. They preach scintillating sermons in plush sanctuaries; smaller prosperity churches have similar aspirations. Men flock in crowds to international conferences to learn of this so-called prosperity movement. Prosperity churches have heaped to themselves teachers who speak smooth words, soothing to itchy ears. They refuse sound doctrine and make mistakes concerning faith. They hate leaders who chase after God; they ridicule passionate people who exalt the Master above materialism. They pant after prosperity, instead of God's posterity. All the while, false prophets continue to plunder the pocketbooks of parishioners like pirates. God is not pleased. In fact, he is angry. Many modern-day believers no longer worship God. They attempt to worship an incorruptible God with corruptible money. For this reason they fail. The gospels depict the poor integrity of people who try to manipulate God. Two of Jesus' disciples worshipped him, along with their mother, the wife of Zebedee. They worshipped him in hopes of receiving positions and authority. Coincidently, Zebedee means gift of God, and women represent manifestation and wisdom (see Matthew 20:20-28). Zebedee's sons, with no doubt, had wisdom about the gifts of God. Whereas they worshipped with the intent of manipulating Jesus. They only wanted what Jesus possessed. So many money-hungry people only serve God for their own personal gain. Prosperity churches approach God with this same deceptive strategy. They worship for money, not reverence. False prophets teach their followers to give, and then expect a physical blessing in return. They pervert the truth. It is far more blessed to give than receive (see Acts 20:35). Most people mistakenly assume that this scripture refers to physical contributions. God wants us to share the spiritual blessing of unsearchable riches. Instead, people who focus on earthly possessions are trying to hit the heavenly jackpot. *"Whose end is destruction, whose God is their belly, and whose glory is in their shame, who mind earthly things"* (Philippians 3:19). Based on the Bible, it is probably safe to say that there is no such thing as an earthly blessing—at least not based on what people generally call blessings (see Ephesians 1:3, I Corinthians 12:1, 14:1, 12).

Committed to the Promise

God promised to bless Abraham's seed and make him a great nation (see Genesis 13:16). God keeps his promises. *"For God loved the world so much that he gave his only begotten son"* (John 3:16). Jesus is the promised seed of Abraham. He was born in Nazareth. In the likeness of God, Nazarene's were people who understood the importance of keeping their promises. In Israel, the Nazarene vow was one of devotion that required nothing from God in return. For this reason, Nazareth marriages were often without consummation or sex. Imagine that. What would you do if your spouse lost a limb or the capability to satisfy you with physical pleasures? Most men and women would probably divorce. In recent years, I met an honorable man. His wife fell ill. However, for more than 5 years, he fed, dressed, bathed and supported her until death. She was totally unable to do anything in return. He faithfully demonstrated his love for her until she died. He kept his vows, despite her disability. This single act of submission makes him more like Christ than most ministers I've met. He kept his vow and expected nothing in return. He could have admitted her into a nursing home, filed for divorce, or even cheated. Instead, he valued and embraced the spiritual significance of marriage. Perhaps marriage is more spiritual than you thought. God gave us the precious gift of his son expecting nothing physical in return. It's time for true believers to submit to God without expecting the reward of physical possessions. Otherwise, physical desires will change your character.

Nameless Nuptials are Meaningless

Some single people live together without marital commitments. However, God desires to separate people from individuality and transform couples into one being (Matthew 19:5, 18:20). Marriage represents the essence of spiritual relationship. Our aim in relationships should be to establish covenant, not physical agreement. The covenant agreement in marriages enable couples to share the same name. Jesus has given us the authority to exercise the power of his name. We are one with him. *"And whatsoever ye shall ask in my name, that will I do, that the father may be glorified in the Son"* (John 14:13). There are numerous accounts in scripture that echo similar words throughout the Bible (see John 15:16, John 16:23, Mark 11:24, I John 5:14-15). This covenant is another spiritual promise from God. At a glance, it would appear that we have been given unrestricted power to change physical circumstances at our own discretion. Carnal-minded casual readers who cherry-pick Bible verses to satisfy their own desires misinterpret this text. They misuse scriptures like, *"If you can believe God for it then you can have it"* (Mark 9:23). As such, physical aspirations are the driving force of prosperity seekers who are supposed to be spiritual-minded. Most Christians, myself included, have been guilty of setting our affections on the wrong ambitions. At some point, most believers have held this belief to their own shame. People ask God for all sorts of vain and foolish things. Carnal-minded folks make futile prayer request. Repeatedly begging God to fulfill physical desires is immature. God is not Santa Claus. We rattle off our wish list to God, and then top it off with, "In Jesus name." Have you ever thought to examine what the scriptures actually mean? Meaningless relationships are unacceptable to God. He considers them unfruitful.

One with God

According to the Bible, people who seek physical things ask amiss. The word amiss is described as wrong, faulty, out of order and improper. Such prayers go unanswered. Unfortunately, when people fail to study their bibles, they make superficial prayer request. These extravagant faith confessions always fail. They are physical and faulty. If we expect to pray in Jesus' name, we must understand the will of God. *"And he was clothed with a vesture dipped in blood: and his name is called the Word of God"* (Revelation 19:13). Most people pray without even understanding the will of God, which is the word of God. *"And this is the confidence that we have in him, if we ask anything according to his will, he hears us: and if we know that he hears us, whatsoever we ask, we know that we have the petitions that we desire of him"* (I John 5:14-15). When we ask for things outside of the word of God, our words are amiss. No man knows the will of God in and of himself. *"Christ has a name written on him that no man knows, but he himself"* (Revelation 19:12). God reveals his word to us by his Spirit (see I Corinthians 2:9-10). When people don't seek to understand or study God's word, they cannot know it. *"Likewise the Spirit also helps our infirmities: for we know not what we should pray for as we ought: but the Spirit itself makes intercession for us with groaning which cannot be uttered"* (Romans 8:26). Instead of rattling off at the mouth like snakes with vain requests, start studying the Bible. *"Be not rash with thy mouth, and let not your heart be hasty to utter anything before God: for God is in heaven, and thou upon earth: let thy words be few"* (Ecclesiastes 5:2). God knows our thoughts while they are afar off. God is married to the believer—we are one with him. Change your request—seek spiritual things. God knows our physical needs before we ask. We should ask God to teach us how to pray.

Asking for Money is like Begging for Poison

Prosperity Churches are filled with followers who pierce themselves with lustful desires (see I Timothy 6:10). They falsely claim that prosperity is God's tool to reach the lost. This could not be further from the truth (see Isaiah 52:3). Money has absolutely nothing to do with salvation. People, churches and businesses require money to survive. However, God does not need money to save lost souls—Jesus paid the price (see Mark 6:8). In fact, we should avoid manipulative people who are poisoned by materialism. Money has an evil influence that can transform human minds. Unfortunately, victims seldom notice the change. An Indiana

186

based pastor shifted the focus of his sermons from spirituality to prosperity. His family, staff, ministry leaders, and many longtime members secretly express their disappointment. However, they were afraid of losing the pastor's respect or their position if they spoke out. Whereas they shout "Amen" during service, and vent their frustrations to those they trust. Unfortunately, this particular pastor has surrounded himself with two groups of people. His core leaders consist of those who can care less and others who are spineless. Therefore, the pastor is unaware of how his change has perversely effected the entire church and community. The love of money will intentionally lead you to destruction. Our ambitions must remain centered on one thing, eternity. Money has a mind of it's own—Jesus referred to it as Mammon. Money in and of itself is not evil. It is the hunger and desire for money that perverts the soul. Poor people also follow the same path of prosperity chasers. Even worse, money has the ability to transform mortal men into idol gods. We must crucify our fleshly desires (see I Corinthians 15:31). Money is corruptible. Lusting after it is deadly (see Mark 10:25). Many wealthy people create illusions attempting to reshape their realities. They pay whatever it cost to keep their shameful secrets safe. However, only love can truly cover a multitude of sins (see I Peter 4:8). Either you will submit to God or money will control your destiny. Money can be poisonous to the soul—God is the only cure. Without self-control money will ruin you. It can never save your soul. *"The Lord hath appeared of old unto me, saying, Yea, I have loved thee with an everlasting love: therefore with loving-kindness have I drawn thee"* (Jeremiah 31:3). God uses nothing more and nothing less than loving-kindness to attract believers. Fancy cars, big houses and plush sanctuaries cause people to chase prosperity (see Ezekiel 7:19). Many pastors falsely teach that prosperity is God's way of giving influence to his people. Integrity is the only form of influence that cannot be compromised. People who honor money more than integrity have forgotten the significance of unsung heroes. Civil rights leaders like Dr. Martin Luther King, Jr. create change with integrity, not money. Just because Christians prosper financially does not mean sinners will come to church. There are many people who do not believe in God, yet they gain wealth everyday. Those that attend church for money messages do so for all the wrong reasons. Poverty is not a consequence of limited faith. Christians who think so have limited education about history, the slave trade, and the economics of a capitalistic society. Oppression is the cause of poverty—it starts in the mind. Making money your priority is like begging for poison. On the other hand, secular society is supposed to identify Christians by the way we love one another (see John 13:35, I Corinthians 13:13, Galatians 5:22).

Ask and You Shall Receive

We cannot effectively approach a sovereign God like a wicked wizard (see Isaiah 7:10-15). Yellow brick roads and streets paved with are quite different concepts. True sons of God seek spiritual things. *"Through desire a man, having separated himself, seeks and intermeddles with all wisdom"* (Proverbs

18:1). The sons of God understand that wisdom is intended to give spiritual insight. On the other hand, we separate ourselves from God through physical pleasures. God only wants us to respond to the desires he places in our hearts (see Psalms 37:4, 40:8, Proverbs 13:12). God given desires are spiritual. The devil infects men with lust. Examine your heart. If your ultimate desire is financial prosperity it is worldly, not godly. God instructs us to set our affections on things above, not things on the Earth (see Colossians 3:12). The love of money leads to false doctrines (see Daniel 8:23-25). These demonic doctrines are exactly what many prosperity chasers purport. On the contrary, Jesus said, *"A wicked and adulterous generation seeks after a sign"* (Matthew 16:4). Men are drawn away from God through their own lustful desires. God does not want our focus to be on temporal things. The Apostle Paul admonishes the church not to focus on visible things, because they are temporary. Instead, he says we should set our sights on things that are unseen, because they are eternal (see II Corinthians 4:18). Without faith it is impossible to see spiritual things. As a result, people ask God for the very things the Bible instructs us not to think about. Be careful what you ask for.

Be Careful What You Ask For

Our short life is not about physical things. What will it profit us to gain the whole world and lose our souls (see Mark 8:36)? *"Grant not, O Lord, the desires of the wicked: further not his wicked device; lest they exalt themselves. Selah"* (Psalms 140:8). Mature Christians understand the difference between what

189

strengthens and what destroys. It is the nature of the flesh to desperately desire more. *"You lust, and have not: you kill, and desire to have, and cannot obtain: you fight and war, you have not because ye ask not. You ask, and receive not because you ask amiss, that you may consume it upon your lusts"* (James 4:2-3). In desperation, Job cried out to God in the midst of his trial. He asked God to grant his request (see Job 6:8). In all sincerity, Job was pleading with God to take his life; he wanted to die. Like Job, many Christians today are crying out to God for things that would ultimately destroy them. Homeless alcoholics beg for pocket change. Drug addicts compromise their dignity in desperation for a quick fix. Carnal-minded Christians are no different. They beg God for money and material possessions to their own shame. Again, always remember to be careful what you ask for.

God Gives Desire

God wants to give us his desire for our hearts (see Psalms 21:2). He does not specialize in giving people the physical things they want. God is not a magician. He gives us desire. People blatantly ignore and misinterpret countless scriptures. Afterward, they conclude that God wants every believer financially rich. *"As sorrowful, yet always rejoicing; as poor, yet making many rich; as having nothing, and yet possessing all things"* (II Corinthians 6:10). Unfortunately, people inspired by the prosperity movement do not understand nor value spiritual riches. *"But God, who is rich in mercy, for his great love wherewith he loved us"* (Ephesians 2:4). Having money is one thing and allowing money to dictate your lifestyle is another.

190

Most poor people already have a plan about how different their lives would be based on money. God is supposed to dictate the changes in our lives. Money is not supposed to change us. People who live life based on worldly riches are distracted from God's desire. *"But they that will be rich fall into temptation and a snare, and into many foolish and hurtful lusts, which drown men in destruction and perdition"* (I Timothy 6:9). We must continuously study and search God's word in order to understand his intentions. Without an understanding from God we will never know what to pray for (see Romans 8:26). In other words, our physical mind, cannot comprehend how to approach a sovereign God. We must humble ourselves. Once we become intimate with God, he reveals his desires. *"For I know the thoughts that I think toward you, says the Lord, thoughts of peace, and not of evil, to give you an expected end"* (Jeremiah 29:11). We ought not take any thought for our lives, which means we should not meditate on money. Otherwise, men become idol gods. As sons of God, we are led by the Spirit of God (see Romans 8:14). The Greek meaning of the word led is agonia. Hence, we derive the English word agony. People who are not willing to take up their cross or suffer for the cause of Christ, are not sons of God. No pain, no gain. Be careful of people who pray for convenience, comfort and capital. Prayers should be rooted in God's word and based on his desires, not ours.

Lord Teach Us to Pray

Jesus' disciples asked him to teach them how to pray. His response is known as The Lord's Prayer. *"When you pray, say,*

SEEDTIME

Our Father which art in heaven, Hallowed be thy name. Thy kingdom come. Thy will be done, as in heaven so in earth. Give us this day our daily bread. And forgive us our sins; for we also forgive every one that is indebted to us. And lead us not in temptation; but deliver us from evil" (Luke 11:2-4). True Christians follow Christ. We ask God for bread daily—not money. Jesus is the bread of life; Christ is the word of God. We need the bread of God's word daily, because it gives spiritual life. We pray for his kingdom to come—not money. God's kingdom is not based on anything our physical eyes can observe (see Luke 17:20-21). Modern-day churches label prosperity the kingdom. This message could not be further from the truth. It is a direct contradiction of scripture. They identify worldly success and luxuries as distinctions of kingdom living. Our personal vehicles are very dependable. Our home is quite comfortable. Currently, we are financially fortunate. It is important to realize two things about the Thigpen family. My wife and I value education. We've worked hard. I've even fought in the middle-east war—risking my life to liberate Kuwait. Nothing we have came easy. We've put the gift of life to good use. My wife grew up Muslim—named after the honorable prophet Elijah Mohamed's wife, Clara. I was raised as a Christian, but I lived as a hypocrite. To credit our religious backgrounds for our possessions would be a mistake—I assure you. As a result of hard work, we have acquired physical possessions. However, don't error in the way of thinking that faith produced physical results. We are certainly citizens of God's eternal kingdom. Our faith has nothing to do with the stuff carnal-minded people focus on in our lives. Allow

God's sovereignty to exceed your carnal expectations. Afterward, your thinking will be transformed from physical to spiritual (see Ephesians 3:20). Only then, will believers understand what to ask God for. *"Thus says the Lord, the Holy one of Israel, and his Maker, Ask me of things to come concerning my sons, and concerning the work of my hands command ye me"* (Isaiah 45:11). The Apostle James said, *"If any of you lack wisdom, let him ask of God, that gives to all men liberally, and upbraideth not; and it shall be given him"* (James 1:5). The Bible unequivocally explains what we should ask God for. *"Ask of me, and I shall give thee the heathen for your inheritance, and the uttermost parts of the earth for thy possession"* (Psalms 8:2). In fact, education, information, interpretation, nor translation measures up to revelation from God. *"Thus says the Lord, stand ye in the ways, and see, and ask for the old paths, where is the good way, and walk therein, and ye shall find rest for your souls"* (Jeremiah 6:16). These are a few scriptures that reveal God's true intentions for asking and receiving. This is the true promise of seedtime and harvest. You can give all your proceeds to the poor or your local church, but without love, it will profit you nothing (see I Corinthians 13:3, Galatians 5:22). It is so important to allow God, not man, to teach you how to pray.

The Excellency of Abundant Life

Without question, it is God's desire for us to live abundant and prosperous lives. Unfortunately, most people don't have the slightest clue of what spiritual abundance and prosperity means to God. *"Let them shout for joy, and be glad, that favor my righteous cause: yea, let them say continually, Let the Lord be magni-*

fied, which hath pleasure in the prosperity of his servant" (Psalms 35:27). Let's take a closer look at this life of prosperity and abundance. *"I have come that they might have life and have it more abundantly"* (John 10:10). The term life is Greek for Zoe. It represents the eternal essence of God. This life comes from God and cannot exist without him. Most Bible students are more familiar with the Hebrew word Ruach, which is the breath of God. It transforms men into living souls. Ruach represents life. Zoe is life more abundantly. Jesus came to bring living (Ruach) souls eternal life (Zoe). The Bible defines eternal life as such, *"And this is life eternal, that they might know thee, the only true God, and Jesus Christ, whom thou hast sent"* (John 17:3). The abundant life that God wants us to have is relationship with him. The definition of prosperity is to excel to the point desired. This is why it is important to allow God to change all of our desires. Simply stated, God will give you a new desire. This desire must be exceeding-abundantly above all the things your flesh craves. Unfortunately, many believers still desire material possession, not spiritual promises. Perhaps we should consistently measure how much time we put into physical things, as opposed to seeking the Kingdom. If necessary, mark a calendar. God is seeking those who seek after him. Do not allow anything or anybody to stand in between you and your destiny. *"Yea doubtless, and I count all things but loss for the Excellency of the knowledge of Christ Jesus my Lord: for whom I have suffered the loss of all things, and do count them but dung, that I may win Christ"* (Philippians 3:8). Without question, it is God's desire for us to live abundant and prosperous lives. This concept couldn't possibly mean what prosperity officials claim. According to Paul, physical prosperity is as worthless as human waste. Therefore, Paul refused to preach about prosperity and other doctrines that have nothing to do with Christ (see Philippians 3:8, I Corinthians 2:2).

Larger Coast or More Territory

Perhaps you're familiar with the prayer of Jabez. Although Jabez was not a king, the Bible chronicles his life amongst the kings of Israel. At a second glance, Jabez appears as a prototype of Christ. He received blessings from God's upon request. *"And Jabez called on the God of Israel saying, oh that thou would bless me indeed, and enlarge my coast, and your hand might be with me, and that thou would keep me from evil, that it may not grieve me! And God granted him that which he requested"* (I Chronicles 4:9-10). Today, Christians call everything a blessing, from high paying jobs to convenient parking spaces. Don't ever forget that God's blessings are not physical. God is a Spirit and his blessings are spiritual. *"Blessed be the God and Father of our Lord Jesus Christ, who hath blessed us with all spiritual blessings in heavenly places"* (Ephesians 1:3). We cannot see spiritual things with our natural eyes. Perhaps you should know that Jabez's name had great significance. Jabez's name means pain, hurt or sorrow. Notice the similarity of his name to the Hebrew word led, which is to say agony. God shows us that through the suffering of his son all men are able to access spiritual blessings (see I Peter 5:10, Romans 8:18, Philippians 3:10). Jabez asked God to enlarge his coast. Most people say "enlarge my territory." The KJV Bible specifically states coast. NIV translation indicates territory. This translation is a major literary mistake. The coast is the land that borders a large body of water. Water represents the word of God (see Ephesians 5:26). Coastal waters, such as oceans and seas, are unclaimed domain. For instance, travelers arriving by sea to foreign countries do not need passports, but foreigners who arrive on land by way of air do. The prayer of Jabez is not a faith confession for physical prosperity. Jabez essentially asked God for more substance; more of what he could never rule over as king. Jabez wanted more spiritual evidence to prove God's eternal existence. Therefore, it is dangerously misleading to focus on the territory instead of the coast. No coast, no water, and no water, no word. Jabez asked God to enlarge the measure of word in his life. The word of God is the only way believers will ever experience abundant life. Instead, so many people continue to ask for more territory—more houses—more land—more stuff.

Seek Spiritual Things

God is a Spirit. The only way to connect to him is in Spirit (see John 4:24). Immediately upon hearing this scripture, prosperity seekers cringe. They feel naked once learning that faith is not intended to produce physical results. For years, Christians have been naming it and claiming it. We've attempted to use faith for houses, cars, businesses, land, money and anything else our carnal hearts could conjure up. Very seldom do Christians use faith for something spiritual, such as studying and seeking to understand God's word. Instead, most churchgoers misuse faith like a magic wand, producing witchcraft and selfish desires. When Jesus taught believers how to pray, he gave us guidelines. Jesus does not instruct us to pray for physical possessions. In fact, he does just the opposite. Jesus actually transitions through eight phases in Matthew chapter 6. First, he instructs us to give in secret. Second, he instructs us to pray in secret. Third, he teaches us how to pray. Fourth, he commands us to forgive. Fifth, he instructs us to fast in secret. Sixth, he instructs us to chase spiritual treasures. Seventh, he instructs us to take no thoughts of our lives. Eight, seek God's kingdom and righteousness. The only thing Jesus teaches us to ask for is daily bread. Remember, bread represents the body of Christ, which is the word of God. We should not go one day without hearing from God. Always ask for your daily bread. The Lord's prayer for believers also states, *"Thy kingdom come. Thy will be done in earth, as it is in heaven"* (Matthew 6:10). God's will is solely based on spiritual principles. Corruptible things do not dwell in an incorruptible kingdom. Therefore, the intent is for believers to experience the evidence of spiritual things during our earthly lifetime. The book of James is instruction for Christians not to desire physical pleasures. Most people have a difficult time transforming their thoughts from carnal to spiritual. The journey starts by seeking wisdom. *"If any of you lack wisdom, let him ask of God, that gives to all men liberally, and upbraideth not; and it shall be given him"* (James 1:5). Hence, asking God to give us wisdom is acceptable. Train yourself to seek spiritual things.

SEEDTIME

The Desire of the Good Shepherd

True believers are not intimidated by people who have more physical possessions than themselves (see Judges 18:10). Insecurity often leads to envy. *"The Lord is my shepherd; I shall not want"* (Psalms 23:1). People who do not fear the Lord chase physical desires (see Psalms 34:9). The creator understands that humans have physical needs, although he intends for us to remain spiritually focused. *"Not that I speak in respect of want: for I have learned, in whatsoever state I am, therewith to be content"* (Philippians 4:11). It is extremely difficult for adults to believe that God does not want us focused on unpaid bills and future expenses (see Matthew 6:25). Remember, God's thoughts our not our thoughts. His plans are to bring us to an expected end (see Isaiah 55:9, Jeremiah 29:11). My 3-year-old daughter often asks for juice. As parents, my wife and I know best. Therefore, my we frequently use milk as a substitute. Likewise, God will place a new desire in your heart. *"Thou hast given him his heart's desire, and hast not withheld the request of his lips. Selah"* (Psalms 21:2). Let's face it. The thirst for money and physical pleasures corrupt Christians. God is not interested in your so-called financial sacrifice or monetary offerings. When Christians listen to the wrong message they produce the wrong results. *"Sacrifice and offering thou didst not desire; mine ears hast thou opened: burnt offering and sin offering hast thou not required"* (Psalms 40:6). God will use this book to cause Christians to see and hear.

Chapter **9**

The Throne of Judgment

SEEDTIME

Never Under-Estimate Your Enemy

It is a common oversight for people to confuse God's power with his promises. When we learn better we should do better. Today is the first day of the rest of your life—make a difference—walk in the promises of God. Casual Bible readers who are thrilled by powerful signs and wonders are often misled. They build premises and then draw conclusions based on unbalanced perspectives (see Matthew 16:4). Where there is no balance there is no justice—be objective (see Colossians 4:1). Power thirsty people also fail to realize that the OT is a silhouette of God's authentic intentions. Silhouettes are clues of something more significant on the horizon. Consider how the serpent is biblically introduced in the Garden of Eden (see Genesis 3:1). Afterward, he is subtly mentioned only four times out of 38 subsequent OT books. The first account reflects how the devil aggravated David. *"And Satan stood up against Israel, and provoked David to number Israel"* (I Chronicles 21:1). King David responded with intimidation to the influence of his invisible enemy. He relied on physical strength. It is important to walk by faith during spiritual warfare. However, King David disregarded the spiritual advice of Gad, his spiritual seer (see I Chronicles 21:9). Gad represents David's ability to walk in the Spirit. Gad's Hebrew name means good fortune. God gives every NT believer a measure of faith. Our ability to see spiritual things is our good fortune. This is the kind of spiritual prosperity that enables us to live in perfect peace, despite trials and turmoil (see Philippians 4:7). Unfortunately, like David, most Christians forfeit sight for silliness. We try

200

to fight spiritual battles with flesh and blood, respond to frustrations immaturely, and rely on what we can physically see. David ignored Gad. Many modern-day Christians ignore God. David, who is God's beloved, measured the strength of his Israeli Army based on a census. His actions displeased God. Without faith, which is the supernatural ability to spiritually see, we can never please God (see Hebrews 11:6). When leaders focus on statistical census their followers focus on emotional senses. Unfortunately, today, many church leaders make the same mistake. They measure their strength based on the size of their facilities and their numerous followers. Therefore, mega-churches are icons in our society. They focus on the physical power of prosperity as opposed to the spiritual promises of God. The entire nation of Israel suffered the consequences of David's oversight—many died.

Pleasures that Pierce the Soul

Throughout history, Satan misuses people—he continues to misuse people—he even misuses confused Christians. When difficult situations arise, Satan provokes, aggravates and influences people to react to physical circumstances without spiritual insight. We can't see the devil physically. Therefore, his craftiness reigns in the physical realm (see II Corinthians 4:4). He operates in darkness, but he masquerades as an angel of light (see II Corinthians 11:14). Without the shield of faith, our invisible enemy wins. Satan is the father of all lies (see John 8:44). For most, fatherhood is an extraordinary experience. Upon conception of our daughter, my wife's obstetrician reminded us that the Y chromosome in males determine the gender of the fetus. As fathers, we possess the reproductive ability to determine the destiny of our posterity. We've been made in God's image and likeness. God's word will not return void, but it will accomplish what he intends (see Isaiah 55:11 and Luke 8:11). As much as possible, Satan mimics God. He manipulates the seed, his lies spread like weeds, and then evil takes root. There is an urban legend, perhaps more of a rumor, that once spread about a nationally-known Mexican restaurant. A cockroach casing, which is the size of a small bean, containing 10-20 eggs, was supposedly infested in a customer's burrito. Days later, her gums swelled. Upon diagnoses, her dentist identified the cockroaches hatching in her mouth. How gross is that? This particular story is solely intended to gross you out. Lies are filthy and perverted. Satan rapes liars of the truth and gains pleasure by those who reproduce his seed by what they say. Remember, you are the head, not the tail (see Deuteronomy 28:44). Take control of your destiny and stop Satan from beguiling you with pleasures that pierce the soul.

Offense vs. Defense

Lies and deception are common practice throughout the world. Satan does not limit his divisiveness to lying tongues. He is the author of confusion—he distorts the truth. God is an author as well. God is the author and finisher of our faith—he wants us to see clearly. It's important to note that professional authors copyright literary works. They possess legal authority over their use of ideas, creativity and literary styles. A copyright reserves all rights to the author or publisher. In essence, an author is one with authority. Satan has authority over confusion, chaos and commotion. The devil allures people into contentious scenarios in effort to steal their God-given authority. We should avoid offense because Satan uses it as a weapon against worshippers. Unfortunately, people who do not study to comprehend the Bible are easily offended. *"Great peace have they which love thy law: and nothing shall offend them"* (Psalms 119:165). Satan wants believers to switch sides. He uses offense in order to get Christians on the defense. The account of Moses' return from Mt. Sinai is previously mentioned throughout this book. Moses destroyed the commandments of stone, melted the golden calve, and made the Israelites drink of the residue thereof. *"Then Moses stood in the gate of the camp, and said, Who is on the Lord's side? let him come unto me. And all the sons of Levi gathered themselves together unto him"* (Exodus 32:26). Much like the children of Israel, people are often offended when their faults are made public. On the other hand, when we learn the truth, we should respond like King David. After the death of seventy thousand men, King David acknowledged Satan's evil existence and influence. Satan is the strategist of theft, destruction and death. David learned to identify the works and power of our invisible enemy. He wrote, *"Set thou a wicked man over him: and let Satan stand at his right hand"* (Psalms 109:6). In other words, an evil leader in authority is the same as Satan positioned in power. The enemy manipulates religious leaders with offense—he wants us to switch sides—avoid living on the defense. Offended people miss out on the true blessings of God. *"And blessed is he, whosoever shall not be offended in me"* (Matthew 11:6).

When the Enemy Uses Your Friend

Among other biblical references, Satan's deviant activity is recorded in Job chapters 1 and 2. Satan is identified as an evil power on a mission. God allowed Satan to tempt Job with death, disease, and destitution. Everything prosperity preachers promise to those who give money are the very things God allowed Satan to touch in Job's life. We must understand the importance of focusing on spiritual things. Job's righteousness had nothing to do with his possessions. Job was willing to suffer for God. His life took a turn of events when he demonstrated love to those who wronged him. His friends ridiculed him. He forgave. Eliphaz means "my god is gold." Bildad means "the Lord loved." The meaning of Zophar's name is unknown. However, he was the sharpest and most philosophical critic of Job's three friends. Zophar's words were coarse and dogmatic (see Job 4:1-21). *"And the Lord turned the captivity of Job, when he prayed for his friends: also the Lord gave Job twice as much as he had before"* (Job 42:10). I also have some friends whose god is gold, yet God Jehovah loves them. They focus on meaningless material possessions and ridicule my relationship with God. Despite persecution, the Bible illustrates love and compassion. Do not condemn confused Christians, even when they criticize you.

Position of Power

God's triumph over Satan is a pre-arranged victory over sin and death. Satan's destiny is defeat. His influence and power will inevitably face destruction in the final battle of Armageddon. The final OT reference of Satan is written in the fourth vision of Zechariah (see Zechariah 3:1-2). The prophet spoke of a high priest named Joshua. Interestingly enough, the Hebrew name Joshua has the same meaning as the Greek name Jesus. They have different spellings and different enunciations, but they are interchangeable. When Satan stood on the right hand of Joshua, which represents the position of power, the Lord rebuked him. The word rebuke means to convict, reprove, reprimand and ultimately to strike at. Satan will deceptively use a display of power to persuade many people that he is God (see Revelation 13:13). On the other hand, Zechariah envisioned an anointed leader. Zechariah envisioned Christ as a brand plucked out the ever-consuming fire (see Exodus 24:17, Genesis 15:17). A brand is a mark used to identify ownership, especially acquired through suffering and worship. The Apostle Paul said, *"From henceforth let no man trouble me: for I bear in my body the marks of the Lord Jesus"* (Galatians 6:17). Paul was branded by God as a result of suffering. *"That the trial of your faith, being much more precious than of gold that perishes, though it be tried with fire, might be found unto praise and honor and glory at the appearing of Jesus Christ"* (I Peter 1:7). Fire represents the heat and light that transforms our sacrifice of worship into smoke. Smoke represents God's glory. You cannot experience the glory of God without suffering for God. The devil cunningly creeps into our daily affairs and cleverly plants physical desires—the lust of the flesh, the lust of the eye, and the pride of life. He positions himself so that physical incidents appear as though they are meaningless coincidences. Since the beginning of creation, Satan spiritually blindsides the children of God. His mission is unchanged. He positions himself as one with power, because he is aware that carnal-minded Christians crave control. God is so amazingly awesome that he does not need to flex his power in order to illustrate faith. *"Then he answered and spoke unto me, saying, This is the word of the Lord unto Zerubbabel, saying, Not by might, nor by power, but by my spirit, says the Lord of hosts"* (Zechariah 4:6). The devil tries to deceptively misuse power to prove himself, and then makes people believe that he is Christ. Satan is a counterfeit—he is the anti-Christ—he works against Christ (see Revelation 13:1-18). The true Christ is the Anointed One. He does not need to use power and might to prove his identity—Christ enables people of faith to see the truth (see Reader Focused Writing Index: *Why God Anoints Leaders*).

The True Kingdom of God

The Bible defines the Kingdom of God as a spiritual government, as opposed to this current world system. The Kingdom of God is invisible. It is not the American Dream. *"Neither shall they say, Lo here! or, lo there! for, behold, the kingdom of God is within you"* (Luke 17:21, also see Luke 17:20). The kingdom is God's domain. Throughout the OT, the Bible provides various illustrations to demonstrate the nature of

God's kingdom. For instance, the victorious nation of Israel is a shadow of the Kingdom of God—only a shadow, a type or an illustration. It is important not to confuse, nor intertwine this physical world with God's spiritual kingdom. Everything in the OT is a physical illustration of God's spiritual plans. If readers focus on materialistic depictions of the OT, they will fail to see spiritual value. Likewise, if you focus on cars, houses and other physical expectations, you will experience a false sense of spirituality. The OT adds to our understanding in the same way that a flashlight illuminates everything in its sphere. A flashlight does not alleviate the effort required to seek and search for objects that actually matter *"Either what woman having ten pieces of silver, if she lose one piece, does not light a candle, and sweep the house, and seek diligently till she find it"* (Luke 15:8)? Effort is still required on our behalf. Our search for a spiritual kingdom starts in this dark physical world of deceptions. This is why we must walk by faith.

A Warning to All Pastors

A mismanaged monarchy leads to manipulation. Absolute power corrupts absolutely. Although God is all powerful, he governs his kingdom based on spiritual principles (see Zechariah 4:6). The meaning of OT names should help readers understand the Bible better. Within the OT, God established the concept of family, priests, judges, kings and prophets. The OT mirrors the NT. In turn, God established 5-fold ministry under the covenant of Christ. *"And he gave some, apostles; and some, prophets; and some, evangelists; and some, pastors and teachers"* (Ephesians 4:11). God uses leadership to bring everyone into the unity of the faith. When power is misused, leadership is perverted. Monarchies start when men rule as kings—monopolies start when men stand in place of God. Religious monarchies are cults. When one individual cultivates the culture of a church, in the name of being the pastor, it becomes a cult. Pastors are not the only men with vision—Christ gives every anointed believer the ability to see—this is called faith. The role of a pastor is to bring people into the unity of the faith (see Ephesians 4:11). Pastors are not supposed to corral Christians like cattle and bind believers with yokes. Instead of envisioning life from the narrow-minded perspective of prosperity leaders, seek the kingdom. Kings are male monarchs over major territorial units. Their positions were often hereditary and their dominion was unending. For instance, consider the modern-day Queen Elizabeth of the British royal family. The continuous list of English monarchs began in 829 A.D.—they intend to rule forever. King Egbert of Wessex defeated the Mercians in 825 A.D. Hence, the monarch was established. Physical monarchies are quite different from cults that psychologically control individuals. Monarchies exercise legal authority. Whereas, religious cult leaders dominant based on oppressive mind-control tactics. Prosperity leaders are spiritually blind, yet they rule based on what they see physically. The king of Assyria, Nimrod, is the first recorded in the Bible. His name means we shall rebel. When stubborn church leaders fail to submit to spiritual warnings, their rebellion is no different from witchcraft. *"For rebellion is as the sin of witchcraft, and stubbornness is as iniquity and idolatry. Because thou hast rejected the word of the Lord, he hath also rejected thee from being king"* (I Samuel 15:23). Modern-day prosperity pastors and OT kings are very similar in nature. In order to put this statement in the proper perspective, the remainder of this chapter will give consideration and clarity to the first 12 kings of Israel.

The King's Ransom

Samuel was the last Judge before the succession of Kings. (The meaning of every king's name mentioned in this paragraph will appear in quotations). Samuel's name means "his name is God." Much like God's children today, Samuel's sons rebelled. *"And his sons walked not in his ways, but turned aside after lucre, and took bribes, and perverted judgment"* (I Samuel 8:3). Therefore, the people demanded a king. About 1020 BC, Saul was anointed Israel's first king. Saul's name means "demanded" or "asked for." Nearly 30-years later, upon the suicide of Saul, David ruled the throne as God's "beloved." David was unable to build a temple unto the Lord, therefore, his son Solomon, did so as his "replacement." In 931 BC, Rehoboam inherited the throne, and "he enlarges the people." However, Jeroboam conquered 10 Israeli nations, all but Judah and Benjamin, declaring "may the people multiply." Rohoboam and Jeroboam positioned themselves in political opposition, much like democrats and republicans. They both focused on the prosperity of Israel, but from different perspectives. They failed to realize that their predecessor, King Solomon, desired wisdom and God merely added the riches (see II Chronicles 1:11). By 909 BC, Nadab inherited Jeroboam's throne. He was known to be "liberal" and "willing." Meanwhile, Asa the "doctor" inherited the throne of Judah and reigned for 41 years. Baasha was taken "from the dust" and murdered Nadab. Upon his death, his son Elah became king. His name means "terebinth," as in a tree. Zimri obeyed God and killed Elah. His name means "Yah is praise." Afterward, half the people followed the "intelligence" of Tibni, and the others chased after abundant "life." Ultimately, Omri ruled. Upon his death, Ahab took the throne as his "father's brother." All eight kings from Nadab to Ahab followed in the ways of Jeroboam. Despite their willingness, humility, deep roots, anointed praise, keen intelligence, abundant life, and covenant relationship with the Father, physical prosperity distorted their good judgment.

The King Inside Every Man

If you are a pastor, it is essential that you exegete the text. *"Therefore thus says the Lord God of Israel against the pastors that feed my people; Ye have scattered my flock, and driven them away, and have not visited them: behold, I will visit upon you the evil of your doings, says the Lord"* (Jeremiah 23:2). Contrary to the special anniversaries, pastor appreciations, bodyguards, amour bearers, double honor and financial gifts, pastors are not God. The scriptures instruct us not to harm God's anointed or his mouthpiece (see I Chronicles 16:22). However, these scriptures are referring to the anointed as anybody who sees what God sees and says what God says (see II Corinthians 11:19-20). Don't ever forget, there is a king inside of you.

Chapter 10

The Responsibility of the Sower

SEEDTIME

They Will Suck the Life Out of You

As long as earth remains people will lust after money. They
will also go to great lengths to acquire it. People lie, cheat,
steal and even sacrifice their lives for financial gain. Prosperity churches are no different. They manipulate scriptures and
build erroneous doctrines hinged on seedtime and harvest.
They distort the truth. *"While the earth remains, seedtime and
harvest, and cold and heat, and summer and winter, and day and night
shall not cease"* (Genesis 8:22). Unfortunately, they misuse this
scripture to teach congregations that their money is the seed.
As stated in previous chapters, the seed is the word of God,
not money (see Luke 8:11). However, there is a physical
seed, which is corruptible, like money. This seed is used to
describe the devil (see Genesis 3:15). God's seed is spiritual
and incorruptible. This seed is the word of God. The physical seed of Satan and the Spiritual seed of Christ have nothing in common but hatred. It is an evil deception when religious leaders trick followers into sowing the financial seed
of Satan. They say plant money, God will count it as seed,
open the windows of heaven, and then pour you out houses,
cars, clothes and unexpected checks. Instead of sowing financial seed, people should simply give. However, prosperity leaders use pressure to influence their members to support their ideas. Their influence is based on control. The late
Rev. Jim Jones killed 909 victims. These people were so oppressed that they could not escape, especially considering
that Pastor Jones used armed force. The thirst for power
changes people. Worldly power is a combination of influence and money. Ultimately, it causes spiritual blindness.

212

Despite these grueling consequences, as long as the earth remains, evil men will suck the life out of churchgoers who fail to study their own bibles.

The Unexpected Harvest

Remember, the concept of seedtime and harvest is grossly misinterpreted. Seedtime is when God sows his word, and we hide it in our hearts (see I Corinthians 9:10). Prosperity preachers poorly interpret this passage as well. Whenever people fail to realize that God's seed is never money they will falsely interpret God's word. The truth is powerful. God gives us his word so that we can demonstrate love to others. Giving money is supposed to be an expression of caring for others. Therefore, the scriptures indicates that God will increase the fruit of our righteousness. The fruit that God increases when we put his word into action is spiritual—the fruit of the spirit (see Galatians 5:22). When God gives us a word to share with others we should not expect a physical harvest. People who desire a physical harvest should pursue agricultural careers. The population of Corinth were known for their wealth. They city is located on a large coastal port. The church of Corinth was rich, according to the scripture.

When we cheerfully share our wealth with others God accredits it to our spiritual account (see Philippians 4:17). Those who understand what spiritual seed represents throughout the Bible, can truly appreciate the harvest (see Mathews 13:30). The harvest is the time when God's word divides and separates. I have a pastor friend who once used an incredibly interesting analogy. During a Sunday morning offering collection, he motivated his parishioners to give by telling them a short story. Ultimately, he said, the only way to naturally stop a woman's menstrual cycle is for a man to plant a seed. True enough. However, he went on to say that some people are trapped in unwanted cycles of debt. He added, "The only way to stop your cycle is to plant a seed." The congregation shouted in response of his motivational ploy to milk members of their money. Afterward, the deacons collected the offering. The only thing that can actually stop an unwanted cycle is the word of God. Fortunately, this particular pastor changed his message when God revealed the truth. Unlike what prosperity preachers say, the harvest is not a time of increase. When a pregnant woman delivers her newborn, the child is indeed her harvest. However, the birth of her child is considered the harvest because it is the time when the fetus is separated from the mother's womb. Afterward, the umbilical cord is cut. Modern-day prosperity preachers identify the theme of the number 9 as birth. They fail to realize that labor has everything to do with separation, not increase. Delivery and deliverance are results of judgment, not increase (see Genesis 3:16). The harvest always has something to do with separation. Farmers will also assure you that the harvest is a time of separation or threshing. Seedtime would actually be a better illustration to demonstrate when God adds. However, we cannot overlook the meaning of the spiritual seed. In other words, we've overlooked what God actually wants to add, which is authority in his word. Instead of seeking the kingdom, most Christians are object orientated. Understand this, the harvest is not when God adds, it is when God violently separates. *"Let both grow together until the harvest: and in the time of harvest I will say to the reapers, Gather ye together first the tares, and bind them in bundles to burn them: but gather the wheat into my barn"* (Matthew 13:30). Are you sure you're ready for your harvest?

Come Out From Amongst Them

Again, God assures us that as long as the earth remains there will always be seedtime and harvest. There will always be times when the fire of the Holy Spirit separates and purges our lives of ungodliness. The harvest was originally referred to as autumn, which means to gather or pluck. The word harvest has Greek origins. It means to cut or divide. The 16th Century Old English meaning of harvest is sword. The harvest is the time when the sword divides. *"For the word of God is quick, and powerful, and sharper than any two-edged sword, piercing even to the dividing asunder of soul and spirit, and of the joints and marrow, and is a discerner of the thoughts and intents of the heart"* (Hebrews 4:12). God's word will make us uncomfortable, unless we separate ourselves from certain people, places, persuasions and things. Prosperity churches today mirror secular businesses. Thus, they can't reach the world, because they are no different from the sinners they try to save. They promote capitalism instead of Christ. Man cannot serve God and money (see Luke 16:13). God calls us to be holy, which means to be separate and set apart (see 1 Peter 1:15-16). Take up your sword and prepare for the harvest.

SEEDTIME

First Things First

Only double-minded preachers hold the twisted belief that seed and money and the same. Do you suppose that the seed can be corruptible and incorruptible, at the same time? There is only one incorruptible seed. *"Now to Abraham and his seed were the promises made. He says not, and to seeds, as of many; but as of one, and to thy seed, which is Christ"* (Galatians 3:16). God made his covenant with Abraham's seed—as in singular (see I Peter 5:23). Jesus is the promised seed. Moses instructed the children of Israel not to sow their fields with mingled seeds (see Leviticus 19:19). Do not mix corruptible things with incorruptible. Likewise, we must not give ear to every wind and doctrine that comes along. *"Beloved, believe not every spirit, but try the spirits whether they are of God: because many false prophets are gone out into the world"* (1 John 4:1). Despite how inspiring some sermons may sound, study the Bible for yourself. Do not exalt man above God's word—study the Bible for yourself (see Jeremiah 17:5). Do not even accept what you read in this book at face value—study the Bible for yourself. If the enemy has deceived you into believing a lie, you have no one to blame but yourself. God is holding you accountable for your soul's salvation, not your pastor, parents or fellow parishioners (see Philippians 2:12). People who lack spiritual focus are cross-eyed—they fail to keep their eyes on the cross. Make sure you're focused on the kingdom of God only—put first things first. Zoom into high definition. We do so, by putting spiritual principles in proper perspective.

Idleness Leads to Idolatry

Again, we are nothing without the word of God. *"And as Isaiah said before, except the Lord of Sabbath had left us a seed, we had been as Sodom, and been made like unto Gomorrah"* (Romans 9:27-29). According to the prophet Isaiah, understanding the significance of God's spiritual seed is critical. Otherwise, we consume the wrong seed, which is physical. According to the prophet Ezekiel, Sodom was prideful, full of God's word (bread), but abundantly idle. They ignored the poor and needy. They were conceited and overconfident, and did things that God himself hated (see Ezekiel 16:49). This is what happens to people who misconstrue the seed with money. The name Sodom means burning. Gomorrah means rebellious people. The men of these cities had burning lustful desires, which caused them to rebel against God. Ungodly desire causes separation from the Savior (see Proverbs 18:1). Be not deceived, just as destruction visited Sodom and Gomorrah, annihilation is inevitable for all men who focus their affections on physical things.

The Responsibilities of the Sower

Spiritual things are unequivocally difficult for carnal minds to comprehend—most are completely impossible. This is in part, why some people do not understand the meaning of the seed, seedtime, or the harvest. They are all spiritual. It is so important for God-chasers to possess an understanding about the responsibilities of the sower (see II Corinthians 9:10-11). The sowing referred to in this book is spiritual, not physical. Therefore, money does not qualify as seed. *"For thus says the Lord, Ye have sold yourselves for nothing; and ye shall be redeemed without money"* (Isaiah 52:3). A sower is a man who takes the word of God and plants it in his heart. Afterward, it produces both fruit and herbs. David declared that he hid God's Word in his heart that he might not sin (see Psalms 119:11). God expects us to be hearers and doers of the word (see James 1:22). Responsibility follows revelation. What God reveals to us he expects us to do something about. The gospel of Luke depicts the parable of stewardship in chapter 16. It took years for me to realize that there are three types of stewards. God only honors one. First, there are those who minister revelation out of commitment. They are obligated until obstacles frustrate their purpose. Secondly, there are those who surrender. With hands lifted and tears flowing they submit to revelation. However, people who surrender are often driven by the emotions of the moment. Emotions change. As I make mention of the third, and certainly the most important group, take a mental note. These are the true heroes of faith. Some are mentioned in the Bible and others are alive today. This third group of people fearlessly navigate through rough waters. They manage to arrive at their destination despite bloody bandages. These are the people who have relentlessly committed to surrendering to God's word without excuse. *"These things I have spoken unto you, that in me ye might have peace. In the world ye shall have tribulation: but be of good cheer; I have overcome the world"* (John 16:33). People of faith have a responsibility despite test and trials.

Water for Sale

Never exchange your spiritual authority for something temporal. This is one of the most distinguishable characteristics of the descendants of Esau. *"Then Jacob gave Esau bread and pottage of lentils; and he did eat and drink, and rose up, and went his way: thus Esau despised his birthright"* (Genesis 25:34). Throughout the Bible, the descendents of Esau, who lived in Seir, continued in their forefather's tradition. They are called Edomites. They sold incorruptible seed for money. Therefore, when the Israelites were passing through their territory, God instructed them to offer Edomites money for meat and drink. *"Ye shall buy meat of them for money, that ye may eat; and ye shall also buy water of them for money, that ye may drink"* (Deuteronomy 2:6). According to the NT, the Apostle Paul confirms that meat represents the complete substance of God's word, which are herbs and fruit. (see I Corinthians 3:2, Genesis 1:29, Luke 11:42). Water also represents the word of God (see Ephesians 5:26). Meat, water, milk, bread, fruit, and herb, are all figurative elements used to describe the word of God. God's word is never supposed to be associated with money. *"Ho, every one that thirst, come ye to the waters, and he that hath no money; come ye, buy, and eat; yea, come, buy wine and milk without money and without price"* (Isaiah 55:1). It is important to understand God's intentions. God only instructed the children of Israel to buy meat and water for money in the land of Seir, because they are the descendents of Esau. Spiritual blessings and spiritual gifts are not actually for sale. *"Thy money perish with thee, because thou hast thought that the gift of God may be purchased with money"* (Acts

8:20). During the time of famine or drought people suffer from lack of rainfall. Rainfall represents God's spoken (Rhema) word. Even people professing Christ, live in a drought when they neglect prayer, mediation and study time. They cannot be trusted. They are destitute. Some popular preachers won't preach to dying souls without financial compensation and other contract stipulations. Unfortunately, distressed, distracted and hopeless people often comprise their spiritual birthright for temporal riches. Esau was destitute. Don't live like the descendants of Esau—we are merely foreigners passing through.

Newborns Require Milk

Milk is an essential substance referenced in the Bible for baby believers. It is considered a basic requirement for all new converts (see Hebrews 5:12). God says that we ought to desire the sincere milk of the word (see I Peter 2:2). Milk is essential for the proper development of the bones (see Reader Focused Writing Index: *Bad to the Bones*). The sincere milk of God's word is what develops integrity. This is why God continuously promised the children of Israel that he would bring them to a land flowing with milk and honey. While milk represents integrity, we will later discuss how the KJV Bible uses honey 54 times to give God chasers an understanding about revelation. Unlike ordinary infants, Jesus was fed butter and honey (see Isaiah 7:15-16). Jesus is the word made flesh; therefore, he did not require milk. In contrast, John the Baptist ate locusts and wild honey instead of drinking milk. He had revelation, but there is no scriptural reference of him possessing integrity (see Matthew 3:4, 11:2-11). John's alleged lack of integrity is what ultimately caused his ministry to be short-lived (see Luke 7:19-28). Milk is intended to build bones in infants. When Christians mature, they should advance from milk to meat. *"For everyone that uses milk is unskillful in the word of righteousness: for he is a babe"* (Hebrews 5:13). Got milk?

Understanding the Process of Maturing

Everything we physically see represents something spiritual—without fail. Everything is created to give God glory (see Palms 19:1, Romans 1:20-21). Don't be so deep that you're no earthly good. Don't be judgmental, but use good judgment. With no doubt, people will mock you. Nonetheless, we must realize that nothing in life is happening by mere chance (see Acts 17:26, Psalms 37:23, Job 14:14, Hebrews 9:7). The word chance is an illustration of free will, not spiritual chaos. We may not understand God's perfect plan or broader vision, but certainly he does. Life's circumstances are not merely coincidental. My mother was raised in the Mississippi Delta as the daughter of a sharecropper. As an adult, I asked her about the process of making butter. She explained, "Milk the cow, allow the milk to sit in the heat for days, and then start the churning process." The churn slowly agitates the cream causing it to thicken and break into butter particles. Hence, butter is made when milk is agitated. Her childhood challenges, as the daughter of a Mississippi Delta sharecropper, help me to understand many mysteries in the Bible. *"Therefore the Lord himself shall give you a sign; Behold, a virgin shall conceive, and bear a son, and shall call his name Immanuel. Butter and honey shall he eat, that he may know to refuse the evil, and choose the good"* (Isaiah 7:14-15). Milk is for the unskillful, therefore, Jesus ate butter and honey. Butter is nothing more than a substance produced when milk is agitated. During a mission trip to India, our group needed interpreters. When foreigners translated our sentences, the experience was agitating. The agitation occurred because we desperately wanted the Indonesians to understand us without limitations. Likewise, when studying the Bible, agitation occurs when we try to understand the thoughts of God. Nevertheless, don't settle for less when God clearly has more. Don't give up so easily when challenges weaken your faith. Don't stop seeking God when the Bible seems too difficult to understand. Keep churning. If you're serious about your walk with God be willing to go through the agitating process of developing spiritual maturity (see Job 13:15).

Honey Represents Revelation

Honey is produced by bees. Honey is a combination of pollen (seed) and nectar. Nectar is a sweet liquid secretion. Nectar is referred to as the drink of the Greek gods. The etymology of the word nectar is defined in the Standard American Dictionary. *Nek* is Greek for death and *tar* means overcoming. Revelation is the only thing that allows us to overcome the sting of death (I Corinthians 15:55). As such, believers possess the promise of eternal life. Christians without revelation are good-for-nothing (see Jeremiah 13:10).

The following scriptures support the fact that bees possess thorns that represent judgment; Deuteronomy 1:44, Judges 14:8, and Psalms 118:12. Judgment is often difficult to bear. The Apostle Paul asked God to remove his thorn three times (see II Corinthians 12:7). However, God's grace is sufficient. God's judgment against Adam included painful thorns (see Genesis 3:18). God's people were instructed to sow among thorns (see Jeremiah 4:3). Paul had no other option, but to endure his thorn (see II Corinthians 12:7). Even Jesus wore a crown of thorns (see John 19:5). Remember, bees produce honey, and you must be willing to endure the painful thorn. People without butter and honey, do not know how to refuse evil and choose good. Milk and butter represent God's righteousness and integrity. Honey represents revelation that enables us to see what God reveals. Painful experiences without Christ lend us nothing more than hindsight, as opposed to spiritual sight, foresight or insight. Allow Christ to reign as Lord in your life. All too often, I've said, "Only if I had known." I've heard others say, "Burn me once, shame on you, burn me twice, shame on me." Nonetheless, it does life no good glancing backward at mistakes thinking about what could've or should've been. Very seldom do people learn from their mistakes or the mistakes of others. We've all seen people who have multiple children unexpectedly; most guilty criminals are classified as repeat offenders; and drug addicts, alcoholics, and prostitutes fall into the same snare as others who blindly walked before them. These are avoidable incidents, but they occur generation after generation. No sane individual aspires to be a professional prostitute. Yet, without insight it happens everyday. Revelation from God is what gives us insight. Without revelation, the devil will turn you out. He will have you turning tricks and doing all sorts of ungodly things that you never thought you'd do. Sometimes, sin happens simply because we don't see anything wrong with evil acts. Other times people have an understanding about wrongdoings, but find themselves unable to resist. We have all been there (see Romans 3:23). Satan will make you turn a blind eye to what you know to be right. You might feel horrible about it in the morning, because hindsight is 20/20. Looking back at life's mistakes causes failure to become easier to comprehend. "If I'd only known," is what most people say after they've made an irrevocable mistake. Godly judgment opens our eyes (see I Samuel 14:29). Revelation from God will shield you from Satan's fiery darts. We must contend for the faith (see Jude 1:3). We must fight in order to see what God sees. Honey represents the spiritual and painful substance that enables us to spiritually see.

Hindsight vs. Foresight

The words hindsight and foresight are exact opposites. The etymology of the word hind is backside, as in behind. The etymology of the word foresight is fore, as in first or forerunner and before. Therefore, hindsight represents the idea of looking back. Foresight is for people who see into the future. People with foresight put first things first. There is a reason God designed the human anatomy with eyes in the front of our heads. We are created to look in the direction we are headed. Otherwise, we are subject to stumble. *"Jesus said unto him, No man, having put his hand to the plow, and looking back, is fit for the kingdom of God"* (Luke 9:62). Hindsight, which is looking back, disqualifies believers from walking in God's presence. Hindsight is 20/20, but it is worthless. Hindsight is not history. They both have something to do with the past, but history is based on facts. Hindsight is based on feelings. When God rescued Lot and his wife from the destruction of Sodom and Gomorrah, he instructed them not to look back. According to biblical history, Lot's wife was so emotionally driven that she suffered from hindsight. *"But his wife looked back from behind him, and she became a pillar of salt"* (Genesis 19:26). On the other hand, foresight is the ability to envision life through faith. People without such vision perish (see Proverbs 29:18). We must keep our perspectives in line with God's. Gospel recording artist Donnie McClurkin sang the lyrics to an inspiring song titled *We Fall Down*. The lyrics are compassionately heart touching— outright riveting. His distinct voice permeates the soul. With no uncertainty, Christians make mistakes. However, the Bible only references the wicked as those who fall down. In fact, the blood of Christ, and faith in God, prevents believers from falling, despite our mistakes. *"For thou hast delivered my soul from death, mine eyes from tears, and my feet from falling"* (Psalms 116:8). I usually enjoy Pastor McClurkin's music, but gospel music should never contradict the message of the gospels. *"Now unto him that is able to keep you from falling, and to present you faultless before the presence of his glory with exceeding joy, To the only wise God our Savior, be glory and majesty, domin-*

ion and power, both now and ever. Amen" (Jude 1:24). Those of us who walk by faith are not physically faultless, but God's sees us through the bloodshed of his Son—this is true forgiveness. The words fall and falling are biblically referenced 250 times. The word falleth is referenced once. *"For a just man falleth seven times, and riseth up again: but the wicked shall fall into mischief"* (Proverbs 24:16). This word falleth refers to making mistakes, not intentional lifestyles. The word fall, referenced in this same scripture, is what refers to sinners who intentionally live a lifestyle of mischief. True Christians are far more than just sinners who fell down and got up. This is not a matter of semantics, but salvation. We cannot afford to conform God's word to fit our message. We must allow his word to transform our lives. Society rewards inspirational singers with Grammy, Stellar and Dove Awards. They especially salute gospel artists who define Christians and sinners alike. When people transition from hindsight to foresight, they become new creatures in God's sight. *"You are a chosen generation, a royal priesthood, a holy nation, a peculiar people; that ye should show forth the praises of him who hath called you out of darkness into his marvelous light"* (I Peter 2:9). Despite Donnie's one flawed effort, his music ministry continues to inspire me. Many other gospel artists are so carnal-minded that they make even worse mistakes. However, I'd like to believe that such an inspiring gospel soloist, as Pastor Donnie McClurkin, is mature enough to accept the *Truth* without offense. The moral of this short message is to encourage Christians to see themselves, and others, the way God sees us all.

Casual Bible Readers Forfeit Revelation

Contrary to popular belief, judgment is not intended to produce negative results. Spiritual-minded believers desire judgment. *"Pleasant words are as a honeycomb, sweet to the soul, and health to the bones"* (Proverbs 16:24). The only way believers will ever learn how to make the right choices is to undergo judgment (see Isaiah 26:8-9, Proverbs 29:26, John 5:30). The Apostle Paul asked God to remove his thorn three times. Again, honey represents revelation. Butter represents the substance that is produced when believers labor in God's word. Words like honey and butter are consistently mentioned throughout scripture. Readers, who do not study, fail to recognize the relevance of many scriptures. Therefore, they forfeit revelation. You've got to be willing to suffer, even as Christ has suffered, if you expect to reign with him (see I Peter 4:1). Casual reading is no substitute for laboring in the gospel. Study God's word. Dig deeper into his mysteries. Keep churning despite the pain the thorn may cause.

Unique Bible Language

It is important to take note of the unique and peculiar language used throughout the KJV Bible. Words like honey and butter lend powerful perspectives to readers who dig diligently. Resources are helpful when studying the Bible, i.e. Strong's Bible Concordance, Holman Illustrated Bible Dictionary, etc. There are websites that God-chasers can access from home. As well as, free internet access is available at local public libraries. For free online exhaustive resources visit www.studylight.org. Also, inexpensive computer programs with complete bibles and reference tools are available at book stores. Christians waste countless dollars on food, clothes, music CDs, and other pleasures. Study materials should always take priority over physical desires. Likewise, study time should always take priority over leisure activities. *"Ask, and it shall be given you; seek, and ye shall find; knock, and it shall be opened unto you"* (Matthew 7:7). Most people lack understanding because they limit their study time and have no resources. Do not depend on preachers and pastors to give you an understanding of the Bible. They cannot give you what they do not have. Very few Christian leaders have revelation, and depending on those who do, it is not God's plan for your life either. Jesus died so that we can all have a personal relationship with God. *"But the anointing which ye have received of him abides in you, and you need not that any man teach you"* (I John 2:27). Anointed preachers and teachers certainly have the ability to edify listeners. However, leaders do more harm than good when they allow believers to depend on their relationship and revelation from God. Pentecostal and Evangelical circles discredit the Catholic doctrine of public confession. However, they are guilty of the same consequence. They too, esteem their leaders above their own personal relationship with God. God wants to speak to you just as frequent and clearly as he does the preacher. In fact, some preachers do nothing more than attempt to interpret scriptures without revelation from God. It is very dangerous when people blindly follow and obey man. God does not want us blindsided, therefore he give us faith—and faith has substance for sight. It is critically important that you understand God's word and see Christ on the horizon. Otherwise, you might end up in a situation like Jonestown—don't drink the Kool Aid.

Dig Deeper and Avoid Lukewarm Water

Seed produces its best results in moist soil. *"And the Lord God formed man of the dust of the ground, and breathed into his nostrils the breath of life; and man became a living soul"* (Genesis 2:7). During a famine or drought, the ground becomes dry and dusty. Certainly your eyes have suffered the frustration of dust blowing in drifting winds. Drifting dust prevents people from seeing clearly. In essence, dust represents mankind. Christians without revelation are easily frustrated—they do not understand the Bible. Therefore, they do not read it. As mature Christians, rooted in God's word, he enables us to become steadfast and unmovable. *"That we henceforth be no more children, tossed to and fro, and carried about with every wind of doctrine, by the sleight of men, and cunning craftiness, whereby they lie in wait to deceive"* (Ephesians 4:14). Sometimes situations suddenly change and we find ourselves in a spiritual famine. I've been there—be encouraged. First, do not build an aqueduct. An aqueduct is an irrigation system for areas that lack natural water resources. An aqueduct is a method of manipulating lukewarm water from one area into another. (Remember, water is figurative of God's word). Never manipulate God's word. Natural water is either hot, in effort to purge, or cold enough for preservation. God promises to punish the church of Laodicea, because they are Lukewarm.

The word Lukewarm is mentioned only one time in the entire Bible. *"So then because thou art lukewarm, and neither cold nor
hot, I will spew thee out of my mouth"* (Revelation 3:16). According to Hebrew study sources, Lukewarm is an expression
used to describe good-for-nothing Christians. Secondly, do
not attempt to bargain blessings for dollars. Churches that
esteem money, or define the Holy Seed as filthy lucre, from
such turn away (see Titus 1:10-11, II Timothy 3:1-5). *"Behold,
the days come, says the Lord God, that I will send a famine in the
land, not a famine of bread, nor a thirst for water, but of hearing the
words of the Lord"* (Amos 8:11). When all else fails remember
this third resolve. Dig. God wants us to dig deeper into the
mysteries of his word. I have a physical well on my private
property. As such, there is never a shortage of natural water.
There is never a cost for consumption. This is how we
ought to react to a spiritual famine, dig deeper into our bibles, meditate on God's word, and invest time in prayer.

Guilty of Treason

There is nothing holy about financial investments, money,
or worldly resources. On the other hand, God is holy. Additionally, he instructs us to be holy, which is separate or set
apart (see I Peter 1:15). When prosperity preachers teach
television viewers, radio listeners and book readers that seed
represents money, they deceive the masses. They twist the
sacred truth with manipulative lies. These men pretend to
represent God and some of them actually think they do.
They make promises in Jesus' name. They swear that God
will abundantly bless those who plant a financial seed. They

say "If it doesn't meet the need, then it must be a seed," and "If you sow into the life of the man of God, you will receive a prophets reward." They mislead blinded followers. As a result, many people think their heavenly reward is earthly riches. Even worse, they describe the harvest as an abundance of physical resources. This concept is a complete distortion and misinterpretation of seedtime and harvest. Their words are blasphemy. *"Do not they blaspheme that worthy name (of Jesus) by which you are called"* (James 2:7)? Remember, God placed enmity between Satan's seed and the Seed of the woman, which is Christ (see Genesis 3:15). Enmity is a deep seated and strong sense of hatred. Christians pretending to love God, but actually seeking money are confused. They adamantly attempt to make finances more important than God himself. Your mortgage, transportation, and even physical nourishment is not as essential as your relationship with God. In fact, earthly possessions do not slightly compare to God's eternal glory. We came into this world without physical possessions and surely we cannot take anything with us (see Job 1:21). *"For what shall it profit a man, if he shall gain the whole world, and lose his own soul"* (Mark 8:36)? During my tour of duty in the Gulf War, an American helicopter pilot suppressed fire on a friendly fighting vehicle. This late-night oversight ended the lives of honorable soldiers. For the remainder of the war, as frontline soldiers, we deemed it necessary to protect ourselves from enemy and friendly fire. The pilot's ignorance, unskilled maneuver, and mere oversight reflected as an absolute betrayal. For this reason, he was removed from the battlefield and dishonorably discharged. He considered the tragedy a mistake. However, it was his responsibility to see, even during night watch. Pastors who pollute believers with aspirations of physical possession are guilty. They ought to be ashamed, discharged and removed from God's battlefield. It is their responsibility to see spiritually. Those who are not skilled enough to distinguish the difference between Satan's corruptible seed and God's incorruptible seed are guilty of treason—stop preaching for a season, and the start studying for a lifetime. This is seedtime. You cannot benefit both sides of the battle; man cannot serve God and money. The wickedness of treason has everything to do with the choice of betrayal. Judas betrayed Jesus. Interestingly enough, he was Jesus' treasurer. People who focus on physical possessions are often sidetracked and distracted from what is spiritually significant. Notice how Jesus foreknew that Judas would betray him, but he never exposed or removed him from the position of treasurer (see John 13:26-29). *"To whom will ye liken me, and make me equal, and compare me, that we may be like"* (Isaiah 46:5). Jesus did not treasure earthly possessions, neither should you.

When Mysteries Make Sense

This section of the book is intended to help diligent Bible students and strengthen research skills. Although some scriptures may appear complicated in the Bible, diligently seek. God rewards those who do so (see Hebrews 11:6). Understanding God's word demands your time and undivided attention. The four rivers referenced in the 2nd chapter of

Genesis are the first biblical explanation of seedtime and harvest. Without revelation readers will never completely understand the mysteries of God's word. Neither will you comprehend God's plan for your life. The biblically defined rivers that flow from the Garden of Eden represent how God's spoken word benefits his people. It is one of the most precise depictions of seedtime and harvest. *"And a river (Spoken Word) went out of Eden (The Presence of God) to water (Give Word or Seed to) the garden (The Harvest or Lives where God Sows); and from thence it was parted (Rightly Divide or Applied), and became into four (Illumination and Revelation) heads (authority)"* (Genesis 2:10). This is how God's word manifests itself in our lives. The Spirit of God speaks in order to plant seed into our lives. We labor in effort to rightly divide or apply the *Truth*. As such, God enables us to walk in spiritual authority. Once the word of God is rightly divided or applied, expected results are produced. *"The name of the first (God) is Pison (Mouth Piece or Words): that is it which compasses the whole land of Havilah (Producing Expected Results), where there is gold (relationship); 12 And the gold (relationship) of that land is good (blessed): there is bdellium (manna or bread) and the onyx stone (breastplate of righteousness)"* (Genesis 2:11-12). God's mouth piece or word produces expected results, specifically for people who are in relationship with him. God's true blessing is when believers consume his spoken word and position themselves in right-standing. *"And the name of the second (Separated or set apart in agreement) river (Spoken Word) is Gihon (Stream or Valley of Grace): the same is it that compasses the whole land of Ethiopia (Blackness or the Place Where we are Protected from*

God's Great Glory)" (Genesis 2:13). When we stand in agreement with God's word we receive grace and protection. *"And the name of the third (Double Portion or Transformation) river (Spoken Word) is Hiddekel (Sharp Voice, Producing Transformation or Double Portion): that is it which goes toward the east of Assyria (Forming Mountain; see Tectonic Plates Shifting). And the fourth (Revelation, Illumination, Manifestation) river (Spoken Word) is Euphrates (Intended to Make you Fruitful, or to make you Produce more Seed, which is Word)"* (Genesis 2:14). God's voice is sharper than any two-edged sword, it transforms and produces double portion. Likewise, God's word reveals or illuminates in effort to make believers fruitful. Notice how the sharp sword, or division comes before double-portion. *"Suppose you that I am come to give peace on earth? I tell you, Nay; but rather division"* (Luke 12:51). Christians without revelation seek addition or increase, rather than division. *"So, there was a division among the people because of (Jesus)"* (John 7:43). Entire churches have been divided because of Jesus. *"There was a division therefore again among the Jews for these sayings"* (John 10:19). Soon Christ will return for his harvest, and he will divide the wheat from the tares. *"And I will put a division between my people and thy people: tomorrow shall this sign be"* (Exodus 8:23). *"Behold, I show you a mystery; We shall not all sleep, but we shall all be changed"* (I Corinthians 15:51). It is important to thoroughly examine the text when studying the Bible. Otherwise, we miss spiritual principles and falsely interpret scriptures.

Chapter **11**

Road to Redemption

SEEDTIME

The Relationship between Salt and Light

God uses figurative words like salt and light to describe
believers. *"You are the salt of the earth: but if the salt has lost his
savor, wherewith shall it be salted? It is thenceforth good for nothing,
but to be cast out, and to be trodden under foot of men"* (Matthew
5:13). The Bible depicts the purpose of light as revelation.
*"You are the light of the world. A city that is set on a hill cannot be
hid"* (Matthew 5:14). Salt is used in purification processes. It
also represents destruction. For instance, Lot's wife was
transformed into a pillar of salt. Moreover, salt is a preserva-
tive. God gives true believers revelation knowledge for preservation. *"The eyes of the Lord preserve knowledge, and he over-
throws the words of the transgressor"* (Proverbs 22:12). The Lord
gives us revelation, which is the ability to see things through
his eyes. Thereby, he preserves his word in us. A Christian
life is supposed to be an open book—not a private pyramid
of secrecy (see II Corinthians 3:2). When people encounter
true sons of God the focus will be on Jesus Christ, not personal achievements. Spirituality is the spice of life. Spiritual
meat requires spiritual salt—the words we speak should be
well-seasoned. *"Walk in wisdom toward them that are without,
redeeming the time. Let your speech be always with grace, seasoned with
salt, that ye may know how ye ought to answer every man"* (see Colossians 4:5-6). Without wisdom we are unable to properly
respond to fellow believers or lost souls (see I Peter 3:15).
When we truly understand God's word we will edify and
redeem based on what we say. Believers who are enlightened
by the truth spice up the world.

236

How to Hide God's Word in Your Heart

As previously mentioned, the seed of herb combined with the seed of fruit is what God defines as meat for his people (see Genesis 1:29). *"And every oblation of your meat offering shall you season with salt; neither shall you suffer the salt of the covenant of thy God to be lacking from thy meat offering: with all your offerings you shall offer salt"* (Leviticus 2:13). Salt preserves meat. We are responsible for preserving God's word in our hearts. In other words, believers must be sure to glorify God based on measuring what we see, say, think and smell by his word. Likewise, we must glorify God with love, joy, peace, long-suffering, gentleness, goodness, faith, meekness and temperance. Your spirit is God's storehouse. When we neglect to preserve God's word in the secret chambers of our souls he considers it robbery. The storehouse represents the place where God speaks (see Malachi 3:10). *"For when for the time ye ought to be teachers, ye have need that one teach you again which be the first principles of the oracles of God; and are become such as have need of milk, and not of strong meat"* (Hebrews 5:12). God's word is spiritual meat for the human spirit. As previously stated, King David hid God's word in his heart. Humans only hide things they value. We hide keys, tools and important documents. These items may not possess great monetary worth, but they certainly have personal value. *"This book of the law shall not depart out of thy mouth; but thou shalt meditate therein day and night, that thou mayest observe to do according to all that is written therein: for then thou shalt make thy way prosperous, and then thou shalt have good success"* (Joshua 1:8). The monument of meditation is where men preserve the word of God.

SEEDTIME

God's Mandatory Requirement For Giving Money

It is unfortunate that most people have misinterpreted, misunderstood, and misrepresented the *Truth* about the tithe. God does not want or need our money. It is not possible to transfer your financial resources into the hand of God. God is a Spirit (see John 4:24). Furthermore, giving money is not some symbolic display of transferring wealth to God's spiritual kingdom. Currency certainly has an important significance, but it has absolutely no relevance to spirituality. God's word has an incomprehensible value when compared to physical possession (see John 6:63). God wants every soul to understand the truth about giving. It is fair to say that his only mandatory requirement is that Christians only give cheerfully, not grudgingly, nor out of necessity (see II Corinthians 9:7). First, you must personally purpose in your heart the amount you want to give. Second, do not give grudgingly. Grudgingly is a synonym of reluctant, resentful, ungenerous, unwilling, stingy and bitter. If any of these words describe how you fill about giving money then you should examine your heart. Afterward, examine the credibility of the source or recipient your money. Third, do not give money because you feel like it is a necessity. Money can never serve as a substitute for God's word. Churches must learn to be more fiscally responsible. Whereas unexpected costly circumstances are met with savings, investments, and adjustable spending. Stop straining the backs of believers by forcing people to feel obligated to give out of necessity. When we do things God's way, we liberate the oppressed

238

"Now the Lord is that Spirit: and where the Spirit of the Lord is, there is liberty" (Corinthians 3:17). When we ignore the mission of Jesus we oppress one group while trying to liberate another. In order words, we take money from struggling citizens and give to other causes. This shifts the struggle from one group to another, instead of liberating everybody. The greater Christian community still suffers. The fourth and most important instruction about giving is to be cheerful (see II Corinthians 9:7). Be a cheerful giver. Give because the source you are giving to inspires you. Give because it makes you feel better to be a part of something great. Give because it is liberating to the soul. There are many other reasons people should give, but necessity and spirituality are not justifiable reasons to encourages Bible believers to give. God is more concerned about why we give as opposed to how much. Only orthodox church officials and prosperity preachers put mandatory percentages on giving. The powerful effect of Christianity continues to thrive more than 2000 years after the crucifixion of Christ. Jesus liberated the oppressed, and he never delivered a message about money.

Why Women Argue Based on Emotions

As Christians we can reform the world—it requires spirituality, consciousness and education. The only way to reform communities is by liberating the oppressed. God uses salt as a metaphor to describe believers. We are supposed to preserve, protect and purify. CNN, and other television news stations, reported on the 2008-09 salt shortages. Likewise, the United States is also suffering from Christians who have

lost their savor. People are turning away from Christianity—
there is a great falling away (see II Thessalonians 2:3). All to
often, churchgoers forget that God has delegated us with
the ministry of reconciliation. Instead, religious zealots
speak with the intent of making money from some people
and making a mockery of others. *"But when he had turned about
and looked on his disciples, he rebuked Peter, saying, Get thee behind
me, Satan: for thou savor not the things that be of God, but the things
that be of men"* (Mark 8:33). Savor spiritual things. Sermons
that are not rooted in revelation are good-for-nothing. They
are absolutely worthless. They do more harm than good.
They confuse excited listeners. People shout amen, dance,
and even cry, but walk away unchanged. Jesus thoroughly
explained the horror of words without savor. He told Peter
that such nonsense causes listeners to focus on the things of
men, which are earthly things. Both leaders and laymen that
rattle off idle words without revelation are carnal-minded.
These are Christians who build aqueducts (see: Reader Focused Writing: *Dig Deeper and Avoid Lukewarm Water*). They
manipulate scriptures. They interpret the Bible to mean
whatever they want. Isn't it interesting that most mistakes
men make concerning the word actually benefit themselves.
They build idolatrous images in the minds of their listeners.
Salt represents destruction when passionate people live
based on emotions instead of facts. For instance, women
must be especially careful. Women are naturally emotional,
despite the fact that some men are too. Therefore, mature
Christian women must be careful not to allow their emotions to control them. Don't quarrel about insignificant mat-

ters. Avoid passionate conversations that have no substance. If you do not have a valid point do not argue about aimless principles. Always remember, your emotions will change—do not allow emotions to change you. Command a positive and productive presence in your life. Control your environment. The man in your life, your children, friends, classmates and co-workers cannot quarrel alone. Don't be rude. However, when possible, ignore unfounded complaints. My wife is a great example of this. As a former principle, she ignored immaturity. As a passionate educator, she ignores parents who make poor excuses. As a loving wife, she ignores me from time to time—this is a good thing. You are in charge of how you view life—it is up to you to walk by faith in order to see what God sees. Your atmosphere and personal aura has a lot to do with your emotions. Your emotions will set into motion various environments, from love and joy to revenge and angry. It is important to live, laugh and love. Emotionally healthy people focus on the right stuff. As the salt of the earth, what matters to God should matter to us. For instance Lot's wife was instructed not to look back, but she rebelled. Immediately, she turned into a pillar of salt. Suddenly, she lost her savor (see Genesis 19:17 -26). She directly disobeyed God. Christians lose savor when we live based on hindsight—start ignoring built-up animosity of the past. The way we feel about the past is not necessarily how God sees our future. Either we can focus on our feelings or we can allow God to save us from ourselves. Salt is the best way to protect integrity, marriages, churches, educational systems and reputations. There is no such thing as a seed offering that has the ability to save a marriage or enhance urban schools. Money is not the solution to the problems we face throughout the world. God does not use money to eliminate world crisis. He rescues true believers from destruction, and then uses them to deliver others from oppression. Lot's wife made her own emotional choice despite God's instructions. Do you get emotionally carried away by disappointments or do your conversations protect, purify and preserve? Use salt to reform the world, other resources will not suffice.

Out with the Old and in with the New

Today is a new day. God does not want the redeemed looking back. The Apostle Paul said forget those things that are behind (see Philippians 3:13). Unfortunately, carnal-minded and emotional people look back at the cares of this world. People make all sorts of excuses not to follow Christ. One man asked to bury his father first. Another asked to bid his family farewell. Jesus responded, *"No man, having to put his hand to the plow, and looking back, is fit for the kingdom of God"* (Luke 9:62). What are some of the things you have put before the word of God? Where do your priorities lie? Perhaps you've silently thought to yourself, "First, I will (fill in the blank), and then I'll start studying the Bible." Do you put first things first? Stop making excuses. Make spiritual things your priority. Lot's wife is a constant reminder of the consequence of focusing on corruptible things. When God gives you instruction, press toward the mark. Don't focus on personal opinions, popular beliefs, or your emotions.

God Does not Want Your Money

Unlike most herbal seasonings, salt comes from the hydraulic method of digging wells. Salt also comes from large bodies of water. We are the body of Christ and we are intended to present ourselves as a living sacrifice. *"And every oblation of your meat offering shall you season with salt; neither shall you suffer the salt of the covenant of thy God to be lacking from thy meat offering: with all your offerings you shall offer salt"* (Leviticus 2:13). Salt is critical in our relationship with God. There are also over 14,000 other uses for this valuable mineral. It is used by meat packers, chemical companies, leather and food processors. It is used in the manufacture of soap, glass, chlorine and paper. It is used to preserve hay, purify and soften water, build roads, refine metals, melt snow and ice, and to freeze ice cream. Rare gold, diamonds, pearls and rubies are all valuable minerals that also come from the earth. However, salt is not known for its monetary value. In essence, Christian churches should not have poor reputations based money messages. Stop preaching about finances and start preaching the word of faith—hope for the invisible. Additionally, churches be known by the grandeur of their facilities or large bank accounts. Beautiful buildings and financial sustainability is commendable. However, loving people who are rich in faith are true Christians. Now that Christ has sacrificed his life to pay the penalty of our sins, avoid unsound doctrines about money. God wants your sacrifice of worship—connect with him. Your money and resources do not remotely compare to the value of you soul.

God's people have misunderstood the meaning of giving for eons. King David had an epiphany and said, *"Sacrifice and offering thou didst not desire; mine ears hast thou opened: burnt offering and sin offering hast thou not required"* (Psalms 40:6). Perhaps prosperity preachers should travel down the same road to redemption. Physical things, to include money, have nothing to do with pleasing God. Sacrifice and offering is not what he requires.

God's Ministry vs. Man's Monopoly

As the salt of the earth, God admonishes us to aid in the care of four groups of people (see James 1:27, Psalms 82:3). When we give to the poor, the fatherless, the stranger and the widow, we demonstrate care for others. However, money is not a demonstration of God's love, but rather the free-will act of kindness. Mission orientated churches do an excellent job helping others. Even still, helping the less fortunate is a personal responsibility. On the other hand, giving to eliminate lack amongst Christians is the responsibility of the entire church. Many churches instruct their congregations to give offerings, but seldom encourage individuals to help others. For this reason, we occupy bigger and better facilities, but we isolate ourselves from those who need God. Accountability and transparency are not required by modern-day churches. Therefore, people blindly give. Afterward, the revenue becomes an untold mystery. God's answer to charity and poverty is not giving to churches. Ultimately, God does not answer the cries of man with money. *"Give, and it shall be given unto you, good measure, pressed down, and shaken together, and running over, shall men give into your bosom. For with the same measure that ye mete withal it shall be measured to you again"* (Luke 6:38). According to the Bible, men are supposed to exchange money amongst themselves. This exchange has nothing to do with faith. Humans in covenant relationship with humans exchange physical possessions. People in covenant relationship with God exchange spiritual possessions. This concept of covenant partnership is popular amongst modern-day Christians. The Trinity Broadcasting Network is the world's largest Christian network. Mainstream prosperity preachers pay for partnership, and then use TBN as a platform to reach the masses. Therefore, many churches, individuals and organizations have become financial partners with the telecast. Unfortunately, the network propels the so-called gospel of prosperity into the homes of viewers around the globe. Therefore, the masses focus on money instead of ministry. Visionaries, Paul and Jan Crouch have changed the face of Christianity in the free-world. The project images globally. TBN's variety, sophisticated programming, world influence, and corporate sustainability is commendable. However, the network sends messages that cause people to psychologically set their sights on physical images and possessions. As a result, people fail to focus on the essence of God, who is a Spirit. Simultaneously, viewers are inundated with images that send mix-messages to Christians who God instructs to focus on spiritual things. The business-minded agenda of excess and greed currently controls Christianity today. Throughout America, we substitute God's ministry with man's monopoly.

SEEDTIME

Religious Wars Right in America

In order to redeem the oppressed, we must possess integrity
and courage. Walk by faith, conquer fear, and then stand in
the face of people who purport financial prosperity as a
means of spiritual success. Contrary beliefs bolster battles
between religious groups. This religious war is between people who preach prosperity and leaders who view impure passions for physical possessions as Satan's bait. These are the
end-time signs of religious oppression right here in America.
Instead of reacting to domestic injustices, veterans like myself, and current military personnel fight to liberate Kuwait,
Reform Iraq, and die in Afghanistan. My Kuwait Liberation
Medal possesses no personal meaning unless America stands
up against oppression at home. If no one else cares about
the way religious leaders psychologically and economically
oppress people American-Christians should. We are the salt
of the earth. Unfortunately, America is suffering from a salt
shortage—physical salt and spiritual salt. For this reason, we
fight foreign battles far away from home—we wrestle with
issues that do not matter. We set our sights on changing the
world and foreign policy, and we never conquer the oppressors who litter on our own front lawns (see I Timothy 5:8).

Actions Speak Louder Than Words

Random acts of kindness and charitable contributions are
supposed to demonstrate care for others. It is sort of like
buying flowers and chocolate for a significant other. The
flowers will die and the chocolate will be consumed, but the

246

expression remains as a caring gesture. Some people do the
same thing to manipulate expected result. These people corrupt pure intentions. The fact remains that God intends for
caring acts to reflect people of faith. *"If a brother or sister be
naked, and destitute of daily food, And one of you say unto them, Depart in peace, be ye warmed and filled; notwithstanding ye give them not
those things which are needful to the body; what doth it profit? Even so
faith, if it hath not works, is dead, being alone"* (James 2:15-17).
Giving money to churches is no excuse to walk by homeless
veterans and turn a blind eye. A church offering is not
God's way of permitting us to ignore the less fortunate. Remember, actions speak louder than words.

Brother's Keeper or Brother's Killer

Money and power without accountability and transparency
corrupts people. This combination often produces a negative impact. This is how religious cults are born. Churches
that are controlled by one man with no accountability are
dangerous. Mortal men become idol gods in prosperity
churches. The apostles were transparent leaders of the early
church, and everybody was accountable. *"And all that believed
were together, and had all things common; and sold their possessions
and goods, and parted them to all men, as every man had need. And
they, continuing daily with one accord in the temple, and breaking
bread from house to house..."* (Acts 2:44-46). In order for people to possess singleness of heart, it is important to eliminate
secrets about financial records. If more church leaders were
honest and humble more people would probably attend
church services. All too often, churches focus on growth

and revenue. Growth strategies are deceptive. It is God's responsibility to redeem, revive, and add to churches (see Acts 2:47). Marketing ploys and other deceptive stunts scatter sheep. Loving-kindness is supposed to be the central theme of Christian churches (see Jeremiah 31:3, I Corinthians 13:13). Instead, we ignore the truth of God's word without even reading the Bible. We allow independent leaders to make up self-serving rules. Blind people blindly follow false doctrines. God does not want churches and Christians selfishly seeking to personal pleasures. According to the Bible, we are supposed to consider others before ourselves (see Philippians 2:1-4). Nevertheless, new-aged churchgoers are self-centered. Even kind gestures are often done with ulterior motives. However, true love is authentic. Even strangers can distinguish between love and lust. There is only one attribute the Bible gives that enables everyone to identify true believers—this is love. *"By this shall all men know that ye are my disciples, if ye have love one to another"* (John 13:35). Love is the luxury all believers should possess and share with others. Our good works are supposed to glorify God, not ourselves (see Matthew 5:16). Otherwise, selfish ambitions will give churches a bad name and chase people away.

Confidential Church Contributions

An innocent and honest church has nothing to hide. Such churches will always demonstrate a premium level of transparency to its donors. The shroud of secrecy regarding religious monetary donations has led to widespread misuse and abuse of funds. In fact, it is common knowledge that many un-churched Americans do not trust preachers. Many pastors are hands-off as it relates to the finances. However, the masses have sent a message that supersedes the reputations of a few good men. It is critically important for Christians to be mindful of how actions effect the entire body of Christ. *"Let not then your good be evil spoken of"* (Romans 14:16). This is unfortunate, because I've encountered incredible religious leaders that refuse to compromise. Greedy pastors are no excuse to forsake Christian fellowship. However, good leaders are hidden amongst many wolves in sheep clothing. Public accountability prevents public humiliation. Therefore, contributors failing to hold leaders accountable are in part to blame as well. The Salvation Army and United Way both distribute fiscal information detailing annual contributions and expenses. God's people are the light of the world, but many church leaders operate in darkness. Churches are supposed to be the most transparent organism that exists (see II Corinthians 3:2). Instead, so many money magnets creep like filthy maggots. They hide the truth in unrighteousness. *"God that made the world and all things therein, seeing that he is Lord of heaven and earth, dwells not in temples made with hands; Neither is worshiped with men's hands, as though he needed anything, seeing he gives to all life, and breath, and all things"* (Acts 17: 24-25). God has no need of anything. God does not need or want our money. Calling an offering "God's money" is just a way of making money and avoiding accountability. Donors should be well-informed about the decisions being made with their hard-earned wages.

SEEDTIME

Judgment Begins in God's House

The Bible indicates that Judgment begins at the house of God (see I Peter 4:7). Even if individuals do not hold their leaders accountable, God himself will make everyone give an account. When God judges, he gives us a difficult decision to make. *"And if it seem evil unto you to serve the Lord, choose you this day whom ye will serve; whether the gods which your fathers served that were on the other side of the flood, or the gods of the Amorites, in whose land ye dwell: but as for me and my house, we will serve the Lord"* (Joshua 24:15). No man can serve two masters; we must choose between God or money (see Luke 16:13). On March 1, 2009, Pastor Fred Winters of First Baptist Church of Maryville, IL preached a message on finance. On March 8, 2009, he was killed in the pulpit when a gunman got 4-rounds out of his gun. Hopefully these two events were physically unrelated. However, judgment always begins in the house of God (see I Peter 4:17). Moreover, God presents us with the choice between life and death (see Deuteronomy 30:19). God gives free will, and we make choices. Unfortunately, many churchgoers have chosen the persuasion of prosperity messages. They've turned to mammon and made money their seed. *"And his sons walked not in his ways, but turned aside after (money), and took bribes, and perverted judgment"* (I Samuel 8:3). Without judgment there is no revelation from God (see Isaiah 59:9). Without revelation, men have no choice but to walk in darkness. The Apostle Paul criticized the church at Corinth because they were faltering in judgment. *"Do ye not know that the saints shall judge the world? and if the world shall be judged by you, are ye unworthy to judge the*

250

smallest matters" (I Corinthians 6:2). When people stumble in judgment, they substitute the Holy Seed with corruptible money. *"Being born again, not of corruptible seed, but of incorruptible, by the word of God, which lives and abides forever"* (I Peter 1:23). They pervert the first principles of salvation, whether intentionally or unintentionally. God will deal with us all. Sometimes he uses difficult and unwanted experiences as warnings to urge others to change. *"He heard the sound of the trumpet, and took not warning; his blood shall be upon him. But he that taketh warning shall deliver his soul"* (Ezekiel 33:5). Sometimes judgment seems questionable to outside observers. Most accounts of judgmental discourse is as blatant as the bloodshed of Christian martyrs. Nonetheless, judgment begins in the house of God.

Why God Anoints Leaders

There is nothing good about the flesh (see Romans 7:18). This is why God tells us to trust no man, including preachers (see Psalms 118:8). Flesh represents our sinful nature. Mankind is inherently wicked. The root of the word wicked is wick. Oil based lamps and candles use wicks as a source for burning light. The oil-base represents anointing. When in darkness, individuals burn candle wicks for light. The oil of the anointing causes spiritual sight. Consider how the field ox is castrated. Afterward, they cannot plow for physical pleasure. They are positioned side-by-side, two-by-two, and then bound and blinded with yokes. These yokes were made of heavy molten iron. This process forced cattle to plow fields in straight lines. According to the Bible, anointing destroys the yoke (see Isaiah 10:27). In order words, anointing liberates listeners by removing the physical blinders. However, yokes are not always bad. Jesus said, *"Take my yoke upon you, and learn of me; for I am meek and lowly in heart: and ye shall find rest unto your souls"* (Matthew 11:29). There is a distinct difference between these two yokes—one is physical and the other is spiritual. Confused Christian think anointing is created to cause people to physically collapse and crowds to react uncontrollably. However, anointing is specifically for sight—nothing else. Christ is the Anointed One. Therefore, he opens blinded eyes. God wants every human to spiritually see what he sees. Thereby, the devil's evil devices will fail. The wick in oil lamps is figurative of our flesh. When God illuminates life from a spiritual perspective it purges us from the works of darkness. Satan's corruptible seed will blind you. The idol god of mammon is the only one who requires sacrifices of money. *"The sacrifices of God are a broken spirit: a broken and contrite heart, O God, thou wilt not despise"* (Psalms 51:17). More importantly, we need light to navigate through God's word. People without anointing rely on the resources of darkness to navigate through life. *"The heads thereof judge for reward, and the priests thereof teach for hire, and the prophets thereof divine for money: yet will they lean upon the Lord, and say, Is not the Lord among us? none evil can come upon us"* (Micah 3:11). According to the Prophet Micah, leaders who lack anointing rely on rewards, hire, and money. Afterward, they deceive people into thinking that their physical resources is the economic security of the kingdom of God.. The road to redemption is not paved with worldly resources.

Chapter **12**

Government Intervention

SEEDTIME

There is a Cost to Go to Hell

There is nothing wrong with financial prosperity. However, money is not God's message to the masses. Most people want wealth. Therefore, the masses are easily persuaded by prosperity messages. God says we should set our affections on things above (see Colossians 3:2). The Bible instructs believers not to lay up treasures in earthen vessels (see Matthew 6:19). We are not supposed to love life on earth (see John 12:25). Besides, the love of money is the root of *all* evil (see I Timothy 6:10). The very tree that God warned Adam not to eat from is the same tree preachers encourage their members to consume. *"If therefore ye have not been faithful in the unrighteous mammon, who will commit to your trust the true riches"* (Luke 16:11)? Carnal-minded Christians describe God's good gifts and blessings as houses, cars and financial prosperity—this is incorrect and corrupt. Our heavenly Father does not give corruptible gifts. *"The blessing of the Lord, it makes rich, and he adds no sorrow with it"* (Proverbs 10:22). The word sorrow in Hebrew is defined as an earthen vessel or something carved or fabricated. In other words, God's gifts and blessings have nothing to do with things that have been fashioned by men. *"Now concerning spiritual gifts, brethren, I would not have you ignorant"* (I Corinthians 12:1). The gifts, blessings, and promises of God are not temporal—they are spiritual, eternal and incorruptible. *"Blessed be the God and Father of our Lord Jesus Christ, who hath blessed us with all spiritual blessings in heavenly places in Christ"* (Ephesians 1:3). Unfortunately, the prosperity message has promulgated through

254

churches on a national level. Middle to low income heads-of
-households usually fall prey to these Get-Rich-Quick-
Schemes. As a result, prosperity preachers get richer and
those who give suffer lack. They use testimonials like info-
mercials to persuade the masses. Whatever a man sows he
will also reap. Giving to get more in return actually works.
*"For he that sows to his flesh shall of the flesh reap corruption; but he
that sows to the Spirit shall of the Spirit reap life everlasting"* (Galatians 6:8). Remember, no man can serve two masters—the choice is God or money (see Matthew 6:24). Believers should sow the incorruptible seed if we expect to
gain eternal life. A ticket to hell is not worth the trip—
redirect your destination and take control of your destiny.

Senator Charles Grassley Speaks-Out

With no uncertainty the church is defamed, discredited and
disregarded because of its focus on finances. However, if
religious leaders refuse to display financial accountability the
government should intervene. Otherwise lives are ruined.
Iowa Senator Charles Grassley, the ranking Republican on
the US Senate Finance Committee has served as a powerful
religious watchdog. When the federal government gets involved its considered accountability. When the King's kids
take authority and speak the word of God its considered
government intervention. The senator initiated an investigation on six televangelists for possible financial misconduct.
His primary pursuit is to discover if religious leaders are using tax-exempt status to support their lavish lifestyles. The
six ministries identified are led by Paula White, Joyce Meyer,

255

SEEDTIME

Creflo Dollar, Eddie Long, Kenneth Copeland and Benny
Hinn. There are many more prosperity churches. However,
Grassley's efforts should be commended, not scrutinized. If
it is the case that prosperity churches are properly handling
contributions what is there to hide? Why is there a concern?
Why wouldn't Christian leaders cooperate and disclose financial documents to government officials? Why do so
many Christians complain about this effort? *"Do all things
without murmurings and disputing"* (Philippians 2:14). Instead of
peaceably responding, one televangelist created a website to
fight against Grassley's effort. Grassley is only trying to prevent lavish waste and the misuse of church finances. The
website, www.believersstandunited.com, serves as a defense
mechanism for prosperity preachers. Even if Grassley's intentions are fowl, truth and righteousness always prevails.
Here in lies the problem, truth and righteousness have nothing to do with filthy lucre and money manipulation. May
2008, sources say Kenneth Copeland purchased his second
jet. The $3.6 million expense was denied tax-exemption, be-
cause Copeland allegedly refused to provide tax officials
with financial records. His initial jet, sources say is valued at
approximately $20 million. Perhaps Copeland is not the root
of the problem. The chaos continues because government
guidelines and church members make men into idol gods.
Joel Olsten is pastor of the largest church in America. Along
with his wife, Pastor Olsten travels the world on commercial
flights. With no uncertainty, his church could finance a jet,
but they haven't. Olsten is scrutinized in countless pulpits
across America, because of his mild-mannered approach. He

inspires people from all religious background, therefore, he receives even more criticism. One thing is certain, Olsten does not focus on lavish luxuries and his messages are not dogmatic. On the contrary, despite Olsten's infrequent rhetoric about Jesus, his lifestyle is a reflection of government intervention. He leads and loves by example. Surely Olsten has his flaws, but money manipulation does not appear to be one of them. Currently, the largest church in America is not the attention of Grassley's investigation. For more information about churches that are guilty of religious fraud visit www.trinityfi.org.

The Barna Group

The Trinity Foundation is not the only organization that exposes religious fraud. Sites like, www.generousgiving.org, Ringotv@Youtube.com, and barna.org are other internet sources that help provide checks and balances for religious leaders. Money, power and popularity are the ingredients that make up the passion of prosperity preachers. Unfortunately, many of these leaders are reprobate (see Romans 1:28). The word reprobate is defined as a wicked person rejected by God, and beyond hope of salvation. God's intentions do not matter to them. They covet money and market ministry. Despite the repeated biblical use of the word reprobate, churchgoers ignore this reality. God will reject people who distort the truth and manipulate the masses. Christianity is polluted with many false assumptions. Therefore, the blind follow the blind. Men who secretly chase money while openly professing Christ are wicked. They walk in darkness.

They hold the truth in unrighteousness. The only way to rescue followers from spiritual leaders who have gone astray is the expose the truth. This is why organizations like the Barna Group are necessary. Otherwise, leaders with hand-picked "yes boards," surrounded by spineless pastor-pleasers, never experience reality checks. Christ is the head of the church, not man. When pastors use church revenue for individual gain they are robbing congregants.

The Corporate Church Overpowers Politicians

Churches that implement profitable practices should voluntarily forfeit tax-exemption. Either a church is for profit or not-for profit. Prosperity churches are fortune 500 companies disguised as community ministries. Unfortunately, unlike Senator Grassley, most political officials are far too worried about losing votes. For this reason, they befriend mega-church leaders, and use their church pulpits for political platforms. Instead, politicians should remember that they have been elected to serve constituents. They are elected to liberate the oppressed. They are supposed to speak on our behalf. Church members are still American citizens. Churches with tax-exemptions are supposed to be non-profits. Why is it politically acceptable for prosperity leaders to profit? The very theme of every prosperity message is about profiting financially—money, money, and more money. Unfortunately, politicians without integrity refuse to stand up against oppression, especially if they are not standing amongst the masses. Mayors, Municipal government, Governors, Senators, and Congressmen have a responsibility to stand against injustices. Unfortunately, many do nothing. Therefore, corruption spirals upward in prosperity churches across America and communities suffer.

The Legacy of Jeremiah Wright

Unlike President Barack Obama's former pastor, the Reverend Dr. Jeremiah Wright, many church leaders oppress. Despite the biased racial views of various news networks, Wright is an unsung American hero. The well-educated, US Marine Corp and Navy Veteran, served as pastor of the Southside Chicago Trinity Church for 37-years. In 1966, he was awarded three presidential commendations from President Lyndon B. Johnson. Wright's journey to black liberation theology started during civil rights turmoil. Wright dedicated his life toward liberating the oppressed. As an honorable American, he sacrificed his life for his country. As a proud African American he sacrificed his reputation for his race. It is important to understand the logic of reformers, especially if politicians and pastors expect to create positive change. In order to liberate the oppressed, you must speak out against oppression. Without the reasoning of radicals like Wright, African Americans would not have transitioned beyond racial discrimination. Without the resounding voice of militants like Wright, there would be no President named Barack Hussein Obama. Any progressive political leader in the Chicago-land area, who is worth their salt, has gleaned from Wright. Any reformer, who fights racial oppression in America, is familiar with Wright. As a student at the University of St. Thomas, (St. Paul, Minnesota) I enrolled in Higher Education Consortium of Urban Affairs (HECUA). Dr. Phil Sandro included in his curriculum a visit to Wright's Southside church. The experience continues to impact my life almost 15-years-later. Trinity was no ordinary church, and Wright was no ordinary preacher. Like Dr. Sandro, Wright was a reformer. Wright fights to liberate the way people think. He has also stood on the frontlines battling decades of racial oppression. His post-traumatic backlashes are not necessarily patriotic. However, his symptoms are the cries of an honorable civil rights veteran. If only our elected officials could glean from a glimpse of his life. Perhaps then, liberating the oppressed would mean more than the personal ambitions of individual law makers. After gleaning from Wright's tutelage, President Barack Obama promised to revive integrity in politics. Hopefully, this book will revive integrity amongst prosperity pastors.

Money Laundering Amongst Church Officials

Instead of using proceeds to best benefit various communities, prosperity leaders live lavish lifestyles. This sort of manipulation starts in the pulpit. When people are desperate, they will go through extreme measures to get whatever they want. Like their leaders, countless prosperity followers are in the business of making money. They invest money into churches, even into prosperity leaders. In return, they expect financial increase from God. Even worse, the money is used for personal luxuries. Much like drug lords, they funnel the funds through legitimate organizations, corporations and nonprofits. Some modern-day prosperity pastors actually refuse to accept salaries. In most cases, this too is deception. While they deny wages, they accept seed offerings. A seed offering is money given to church leaders. Whereas, members expect to get physical possessions from God in return. I have a reformed pastor friend who describes how some religious leaders hustle their own churches for money. They allow guest preachers to speak at their churches for cash love offerings. In return their co-harts do the same for them. This behavior continues throughout the year. Afterward, these preachers make upward of $20,000 in non-reportable or untraceable income. Making extra money is not the problem. However, deceiving people in order to increase your wages is wicked. The hustle is successful because most modern-day Christians give in order to gain. Churchgoers gamble with America's biggest shysters, who are prosperity pastors. As for those who refuse weekly salaries, while this seems commendable at a glance, it is not. It is only about image. It is a part of their marketing shenanigans. They do not accept salaries, but they accept large financial gifts, expense accounts, credit cards, houses, cars, travel and seed offerings. The federal government, i.e. the Internal Revenue Service and Senate Finance Committee, do not recognize the religious rhetoric that conceals such deception. This is why investigations are necessary. It is especially difficult to identify these manipulative transfer of funds when the transactions are made with cash. Therefore, large payments are funneled through tax-exempt churches and labeled as honorariums and gifts. This is how prosperity pastors manipulate the system and avoid luxury taxes, but live luxurious lifestyles. Meanwhile, those who are tricked into thinking they can purchase hope with dollar bills are cheated by church leaders.

The Sole Proprietorship of Prosperity Pastors

Sole proprietorship is an extreme horror of modern-day prosperity churches, especially where the church founder is the pastor. One man with exclusive rights to the charitable resources is dangerous. Money and power without accountability is often problematic, such as in monarchies. On the other hand, democracies are about checks and balances, despite its imperfections. Spiritual leadership diminishes when prosperity pastors are consumed with ownership. In effort to sustain financial success, ownership demands a sense of control. Only Christ is in control of the true church. When one man is in charge of a church facility, without an active board, he becomes an oppressor. This is why pastors should avoid sole proprietorship. There are threats involved with trying to be in control of religious groups. Mortal men are not intended to become idol gods. In essence, we are not in control, God is. Therefore, we must learn to trust the Lord. Since mankind has no monopoly on control money-hungry people manipulate in order to gain expected results. Hence, prosperity preachers lie, deceive, and swindle followers. They misuse scriptures to market their agendas. The concept is similar to McDonald's, Burger King, and other unhealthy, but tasty, fast food marketing strategies. Television commercials, bill-board displays, and radio advertisement only disclose what they want consumers to know. Likewise, sole proprietors in church pulpits only mention scriptures they want listeners to hear. In both cases, fast foods and the sole proprietorship of pastors are psychologically unhealthy.

Satan's Purpose Driven Attack on Faith

Satan's ultimate scheme is to deceive people into focusing on themselves. His plot has not changed since the beginning of creation. *"And the serpent said unto the woman, ye shall not surely die: For God doth know that in the day ye eat thereof, then your eyes shall be opened, and ye shall be as gods, knowing good and evil"* (Genesis 3:4-5). Adam and Eve listened to Satan's message, changed their perceptions, consumed Satan's seed, focused on themselves, and spiritually died. Satan wants us to focus on self-fulfillment. According to the prophets Isaiah and Ezekiel, the devil's fall from eternity was based on his ambition for personal greatness. Furthermore, he tempted Jesus based on physical needs (see Matthew 4:3). Satan's message is no different today. Therefore, any religious doctrine that causes Christians to focus on themselves is dangerous. God must remain the focus of our faith. Over the past century, American churches have gone through several distinct shifts. The move of God during the Azusa Street Revival caused people to focus on the Holy Ghost. Soon after, the church transitioned to the word of faith movement, which utilizes faith as a means of producing physical

263

things. For this reason, individuals tried to define their own purpose driven movement that refocused faith on physical results. Today, prosperity preachers claim that money is God's seed. Therefore, many Christians have become consumed with earthly affections. The progression of the 20th-21st Century Church mirrors Adam and Eve's experience. Rick Warren's book, The Purpose Driven Life, sold more than 25-million copies. People have itchy ears for messages about self-fulfillment. Many churches have changed their perception and commitment to holiness. Moreover, the prosperity movement has encouraged a nation of churches to consume Satan's seed of physical wealth. Again, the church is focused on earthly affections and many Christians are spiritually dying. The true message of the gospel is good news about Christ, not you. Stop searching to discover who you are. Stop setting your affections on earthly possessions. Seek the Lord while he may be found.

Marketing Churches and Forgetting Christ

New-aged prosperity churches have become so consumed with marketing facilities that Christ is often overlooked. They promote inspiration sensation without revelation. In prosperity churches, evangelism is considered basketball tournaments, car shows, shopping sprees and other secular events that earn money. People who make money a priority forget to chase what actually matters. Christ and the cross is no longer the theme of these churches. The love of money is rooted deep in the hearts of people who set their affections on the wrong thing. For this reason, finances is the leading cause of divorce in America. Even worse, more than 50-percent of all Christian marriages end in divorce. This is because money is the theme of modern-day churches. According to the Bible, money as an idol god named mammon (see Matthew 6:24). Money has the deceptive ability to degrade the way we think. It causes   divorce, crime, violence, fraud, theft, deception, manipulation and every other form of corruption. Prosperity churches market fancy facilities, mainstream speakers, and extravagant events. The marketing strategy of many modern-day churches is suffocating the cross of Christ. We should learn from the mistakes and highway robbery of cooperate extortionists. Whereas, America is treading dangerous waters trying to escape the 2008-09 economic recession. Sometimes, survivors must suffer serious losses in order to see a spiritual perspective. Some people lose everything before they realize what actually matters. I'm reminded of the friend I initially referenced in the biographical excerpt of this book, Ernest Googe. The improper diagnoses of a common cold led to an even worse case scenario. Don't undermine the perverse affects of America's religious prosperity movement. People who make money a priority forget to chase what actually matters. When it was clear that Ernest's circumstances were a matter of life or death, money suddenly became meaningless. Likewise, the Body of Christ needs a heart transplant. *"For whosoever will save his life shall lose it; and whosoever will lose his life for my sake shall find it"* (Matthew 16:25). Religion cannot afford to focus wealth and forget about Christ. Make today the beginning of your commitment to chase what matters to God.

SEEDTIME

How to Study the Bible

Appendix A

An Exegetical Appendix

SEEDTIME

9-Step Exegetical Process

To mathematically divide something is to systematically break it down into various portions. This means it is important to take one part of the Bible and measure its validity by using another part. This process is called an exegesis. An exegetical statement includes historical, grammatical, literary, and contextual explanations. This exegetical process is a detailed analytical study of scripture. It is close analysis of a text to discover the authors original intent. It enables readers to effectively answer one primary question, "What did the text originally mean?" The final step in any exegetical process should always include a concept called hermeneutics. This step turns an ancient Bible into an invaluable modern-day resource. It is also intended to answer one question, "How do the scriptures apply to us today?"

Step 1. Select a passage and identify the context, i.e. *What comes before it and what comes after it?*
Step 2. Examine line by line to identify the form, i.e. *Is it a prayer, parable, speeches, genealogy?*
Step 3. Identify the themes, i.e. *Christology , parallel. What other biblical theme is the text giving reference to?*
Step 4. Identify the sources, i.e. Who wrote the text and who is the text about?
Step 5. Examine the form, i.e. *evaluate the literary context; language, essay, poetry, history, prophecy.*
Step 6. Examine the significance of words, i.e. *the writers authentic style of ministry.*
Step 7. Determine the major focus of the text, i.e. *moral or meaning.*
Step 8. Determine the Sitz im Leben, i.e. *setting in life.*
Step 9. Determine the theological dimension, i.e. the summary, hermeneutics; "How do the scriptures apply to us today?"

Exhaustive Glossary

Appendix B

Understanding
Biblical Metaphors
and Figurative Language

SEEDTIME

Glossary Instructions

The Bible often uses figurative language. In order for readers to understand spiritual things, it is important to cross reference scriptures, carefully examine word usage, etymology, and study the context. Otherwise, the meaning of the Bible is diluted when readers fail to understand. The following unique explanations will help you identify with terms used throughout this book and the Bible. For traditional and supportive definitions refer to a Webster's Dictionary, Bible Dictionary, Encyclopedia, or On-line Sources. (The number listed next to the key word in parenthesis indicates how many times the word is used throughout the Bible). This word reference is a phenomenal tool for individuals learning to study scripture. It will also help Bible students make since out of metaphors mentioned from Genesis to Revelation. The details provided throughout this book, including the *Glossary*, are intended to provide God-chasers with nothing more than a better understanding. However, it is important to search God's word until he reveals himself to you. Information, education, translations and interpretations are intended to guide you to revelation. God is real. Until God personally reveals himself to you keep seeking. The Bible itself, this book, and no other can replace or substitute a personal relationship with God himself. Despite how inspirational and influential powerful men may be, it is important for God to become a living and breathing reality in your life. Otherwise, men become idol gods. Use this word reference to learn how to identify figurative language that endures the test of time.

Glossary

A

Authority: (34)   The root word author suggests ownership, possession, or right.

B

Bee: (4)   Also see bees, with stingers like *thorn* suggesting judgment; bees attack only when they feel the need to protect the queen (see woman or wisdom), also it's honey; an insect that uses pollen and nectar to produce honey.

Blood: (375)   Symbolic of life producing power and its ability to be transferred.

Bread: (329)   Represents of God's word that Jesus instructs us to partake of daily.

Butter: (10)   A meaningful substance produced when ever *milk* is agitated.

Bone: (101)   Also see bones; indicative of integrity.

C

Cloud: (141)   Also see clouds; the manifestation or that which veils God's glory.

Cold: (17)   Important for preservation; God's desire for his people.

Cattle: (133)   Cow, milk producing beast or animal.

Chariot: (154)   Represents a transition from one place to another—change. See Ezekiel's wheel.

SEEDTIME

D

Day: (2619) Also see days, day's, days', daytime, daysrping and daysman; light, illumination, and revelation.

Darkness: (142) Indicates where the lesser light or moon rules; night.

F

Faith: (231) Proof of things that cannot be seen.

Fire: (506) Important for purging; also represents destruction; heat or hot.

Fig: (60) Also see figs; *fruit* grown from seed mixed with multiple plant or herbal species; represents power in God's word.

Fruit: (221) Also see fruits; spiritual supplement identified in the word (seed) as love, joy, peace, longsuffering, gentleness, goodness, faith, meekness, and temperance; fruit represents what gives God glory.

G

Garment: (170) Also see garments; clothing defines one's possessions or authority

Glory: (371) The face, light, or brightness of God. What believers are supposed to seek.

Gold: (356) Signifies relationship, see gold chains, golden idols, golden crowns, etc...

Grain: (7) Natural or raw ingredients used to make *bread*.

H

Herb: (37)   Also see herbs; spiritual supplement
                 identified in the word (seed) judgment;
                 also intended to benefit believers; herbs
                 represent what gives man glory; herbs are
                 used to appeal to the senses of humans; as
                 a result of herbs we have spices for taste,
                 natural medicines for health, brilliant
                 colors for beauty, and fragrance for
                 perfumes.

Honey: (54)   Sweet syrup naturally produced by bees;
                 symbolic of revelation, the sweet
                 taste of God's presence or word.

Horse: (298)   Also see horses, ass, mule; represents
                 change which is produced by the
                 glory of God; symbolic of corporate
                 change.

Hot: (60)   Also see heat, necessary for purging; God's
                 desire for his people.

Harvest: (53)   Sickle or sharp sword – represents the time
                 when God's word divide; Also
                 see Autumn – to gather and to pluck.

L

Light: (277)   Important component of speed and sound;
                 day; signified by the greater light or sun.

Lukewarm: (1)   Aqueduct used to *force or manipulate* water
                 to produce specific results.

SEEDTIME

M

Meat: (282)   Also see meats; necessary for sacrifice; defined by seed of herbs and seed of fruit combined; the complete substance of God's word.

Might: (436)   Superior power of strength; actual force; different from power and strength.

Milk: (48)   Used to describe basic Bible principles needed to sustain newly born again Believers; identified as sincere milk of the word.

Mountain: (553)   Also see mountains, hills, and high place; place of worship.

N

Naked: (45)   Uncovered; without authority or fully submitted.

Nectar: (0)   Not used in the Bible; however, bees need it to produce honey, which is referenced 54 times; it is the sweet juice inside the stems of plants; nectar is referred to as the drink of the Roman and Greek gods; the Greek etymology of the word is nek which means death, and tar which means overcoming.

Night: (310)   Darkness; confusion, lack of understanding.

O

Oil: (187)   Represents the suffering required to pro-
                duce the primary ingredient to anointing;
                olive must be beaten or pressed in order to
                extract oil; indicates a painful process;
                anointing oil represent that which gives
                sight; see candles, yokes, and sin sick souls.

Ox: (52)   Castrated cattle intended to slowly produce
                change or discipline; represents how peo-
                ple change.

P

Prophet: (453)   God's mouth piece.

Pollen: (0)   Not used in the Bible; however, bees need
                it to produce honey, which is referenced
                54 times; it is a seed based or fertilizing
                elements for flowering plants.

Power: (259)   The ability to do or act; uniquely different
                from strength and might.

R

Rest: (265)   To be quiet.

Rivers: (217)   Flowing *water*.

Rock: (128)   Figurative of revelation; Jesus is the rock.

Rain: (87)   Represents God's method of dispersing his
                word.

Rate: (5)   The amount of glory a person can with
                stand; the ingredients of glory.

Red: (49)   Represents power intended to be seen.

Revelation: (18)   Also see revelations and reveal; to see the
                      spiritual things of God.

S

Seed: (258)   Also see seeds; represent the word of
                      God.

Seedtime: (1)   The season when God sows his seed or
                      word; to become pregnant.

Silver: (281)   Symbolizing redemption.

Soil: (1)   The word is used in a singular tense; soil is
                      indicative of the human heart or spirit.

Stone: (332)   Also see stones; hewn out of larger rocks;
                      often refined or smooth; stones
                      also represent revelation; Christians are
                      supposed to be lively stones; Jesus is the
                      chief corner stone.

Storehouse: (2)   A shelter used to harvest crops and protect
                      them from extreme weather.

Strength: (230)   The quality or state of being strong;
                      essence, presence, uniquely different
                      from power and might.

Spices: (29)   Ingredients needed for anointing oil;
                      representing different qualities and/or
                      attributes.

Summer: (27)   Time of rest; longer days.

T

Tithe: (32)   Also see tithes; One tenth part, especially as offered to God; an omer is a tenth part of an ephah, which is dry *grain*; meat.

Thistle: (6)   Also see thistle; judgment produced by wood which represents spirit.

Thorns: (54)   Also see thorns; Represents pain and suffering produced by judgment; the only way to manifest revelation; see Jesus' crown of thorns and the thorn in Paul's flesh.

W

Water: (613)   Also see waters; a cleansing agent; figurative of God's word.

Weakness (7)   Frailties, sickness, infirmities resulting from nakedness; that which enables God's strength or glory to be made perfect.

White: (66)   Righteousness, purity, and holiness.

Wine: (215)   Also see wines; produced from the fruit of the vine; symbolic of power; often misused.

Winter: (13)   Time of protection; longer hair, hibernation, manifestation of the word.

Wood: (132)   The manifestation of seed; possesses the capability to burn (make fire); bees put their honeycombs in the trees; Christians are supposed to be like trees planted by the *rivers of water*.

Woman: (2196)   Also see women, she, and her; Symbol of

wisdom.

Worship: (100)   To kiss; to become intimately connected with.

Wrestle: (4)   To convince or persuade; to sway the thinking of another.

Reader-Focused-Writing Index

Appendix C

Quick Reference Navigational Tool

SEEDTIME

Reader-Focused-Writing Index
Quick Reference Navigational Tool

The Masquerade of Monstrous Men
Power enables believers to liberate the world of oppression. Find out how the devil manipulates people out of power and uses it against the kingdom of God.

SEEDTIME

Proof of Promises Eyes Cannot See

Revolutionize your way of thinking about the fundamental principle of faith. Contrary to popular belief, faith enables Christians to see. It is not a magic wand to get rich quick.

Perilous Pitfalls of Prosperity Preachers

Gain a foundational overview of how prosperity effects Christianity. Quickly go behind the scenes and discover the truth about the poisonous plague of the prosperity theology.

Chapter 5, pg. 105

SEEDTIME

Memoirs of Merchants

Dig deep into the historical context of the Bible and learn the culture, language, and context of important patriarchs. Trace the truth concerning the history of the tithe.

Chapter 6, p. 137

The Perfect Crime

Learn the marketing strategies that make modern-day church much like casinos. Gain a greater understanding about OT animal sacrifices and God's religious expectations.

Chapter 7, p. 165

Eternal Desire

We need God for everything, but instead of asking for anything, first, see what God has to say about your prayer life. Gain a new desire.

Chapter 8, p. 179

SEEDTIME

The Throne of Judgment

Money has always been mankind's greatest temptation. The kingdom of God is not the American Dream—one is spiritual and the other is physical. Allow God to reveal his spiritual kingdom to you.

Chapter 9, p. 199

The Responsibility of the Sower

The Bible is complete with metaphors and figurative language. As a result, it is filled with God's secrets. God's word is the seed. Learn what he expects us to do with it.

Road to Redemption

God sends judgment to get us on the right track—open your eyes.

SEEDTIME

Government Intervention

Learn the importance of liberating the oppressed. Learn why the prosperity theology is oppressive. Gain an overview of how the currency of this current government is effecting the church.

The Truth About Financial Prosperity

APENDIX D

An Appendix of Biblical Economics

SEEDTIME

The Truth About Financial Prosperity

The relevance of this appendix is to empower readers with an extensive resource of biblical economics. This section explores the scriptural use of 13-words used throughout the Bible. Each word lends readers a better understanding of God's perspective concerning money. The words are chronologically listed in reference to there relationship to financial gain. The words are money; riches; wealth; greed; affections; contentment; reward; vanity; thoughts; spiritual gifts; give; treasures; and oppression. Scriptures are independently referenced throughout this appendix. The italicized portion of the scripture indicates the significance of the entry as it relates to prosperity. This section also proves that God's word is not subject for personal interpretation. When readers rightly divide God's word with other relevant and supportive scriptures the Bible interprets itself. Our opinions, theories and personal feelings are not effective means to understand God's intentions. This appendix is titled *Biblical Economics* because it gives readers an overview of God's outlook on money matters. Readers will gain a detailed and descriptive view of the financial prosperity theology.

An Appendix of Biblical Economics

Affections

"And they that are Christ's have *crucified the flesh with the affections* and lusts" (Galatians 5:24).

"*Set your affection on things above,* not on things on the earth" (Colossians 3:2)

"Teaching us that, *denying ungodliness and worldly lusts,* we should live soberly, righteously, and godly, in this present world" (Titus 2:12).

"Whose end is destruction, whose God is their belly, and whose glory is in their shame, *who mind earthly things*" (Philippians 3:19).

Contentment

"But godliness with *contentment is great gain*" (I Timothy 6:6).

"And he said unto them, Do violence to no man, neither accuse any falsely; *and be content with your wages*" (Luke 3:14).

"Not that I speak in respect of want: for I have learned, *in whatsoever state I am, therewith to be content*" (Philippians 4:11).

"And having food and raiment *let us be therewith content*" (I Timothy 6:8).

"Let your conversation *be without covetousness; and be content* with such things as ye have: for he hath said, I will never leave thee, nor forsake thee" (Hebrews 13:5).

SEEDTIME

Give

"Remove far from me vanity and lies: *give me neither poverty nor riches;* feed me with food convenient for me" (Proverbs 30:8).

"*The horseleach hath two daughters, crying , Give, give.* There are three things that are never satisfied, yea , four things say not, It is enough" (Proverbs 30:15).

"*Or what shall a man give in exchange for his soul*" (Mark 8:37)?

"And though I bestow all my goods to feed the poor, *and though I give my body to be burned, and have not charity, it profiteth me nothing*" (I Corinthians 13:3).

"Meditate upon these things; *give thyself wholly to them; that thy profiting may appear to all*" (I Timothy 4:15).

"Every man according as he purposeth in his heart, so let him *give; not grudgingly, or of necessity:* for God loveth a cheerful giver" (II Corinthians 9:7).

"*Give, and it shall be given unto you, good measure, pressed down, and shaken together, and running over, shall men give into your bosom.* For with the same measure that ye mete withal it shall be measured to you again" (Luke 6:38).

Greed

"Woe unto them! for they have gone in the way of Cain, *and ran greedily after the error of Balaam for reward,* and perished in the gainsaying of Korah" (Jude 1:11)

"In thee have they taken gifts to shed blood; thou hast taken usury and increase, *and thou hast greedily gained of thy neighbors by extortion*, and hast forgotten me, saith the Lord God" (Ezekiel 22:12).

"*So are the ways of every one that is greedy of gain; which* taketh away the life of the owners thereof" (Proverbs 1:19).

"*He that is greedy of gain troubleth his own house;* but he that hateth gifts shall live" (Proverbs 15:27).

"*Yea, they are greedy dogs which can never have enough,* and they are shepherds that cannot understand: they all look to their own way, every one for his gain, from his quarter" (Isaiah 56:11).

"Likewise must the deacons be grave, not double-tongued, not given to much wine, *not greedy of filthy lucre*" (I Timothy 3:8).

Money

"Are we not counted of him strangers? for he hath sold us, and hath quite *devoured also our money*" (Genesis 31:15).

"And when money failed in the land of Egypt, and in the land of Canaan, all the Egyptians came unto Joseph, and said, Give us bread: for why should we die in thy presence? for the *money fails*" (Genesis 47:15).

"*And the priests consented to receive no more money of the people*, neither to repair the breaches of the house" (II Kings 12:8).

"*He that putteth not out his money to usury*, nor taketh reward against the innocent. He that doeth these things shall never be moved" (Psalms 15:5).

Money continued

"For wisdom is a defense, and *money is a defense*: but the excellency of knowledge is, that wisdom giveth life to them that have it" (Ecclesiastes 7:12).

"For thus saith the LORD, Ye have sold yourselves for naught; and *ye shall be redeemed without money*" (Isaiah 52:3).

"But Peter said unto him, *Thy money perish with thee*, because thou hast thought that the gift of God may be purchased with money" (Acts 8:20).

"For the *love of money is the root of all evil*: which while some coveted after, they have erred from the faith, and pierced themselves through with many sorrows" (I Timothy 6:10).

"The heads thereof judge for reward, and the priests thereof teach for hire, *and the prophets thereof divine for money: yet will they lean upon the LORD*, and say, Is not the LORD among us? none evil can come upon us" (Micah 3:11).

"No man can serve two masters: for either he will hate the one, and love the other; or else he will hold to the one, and despise the other. *Ye cannot serve God and mammon*" (Matthew 6:24).

Oppression

"*He delivereth the poor in his affliction, and openeth their ears in oppression*" (Job 36:15).

"Learn to do well; seek judgment, *relieve the oppressed,* judge the fatherless, plead for the widow" (Isaiah 1:17).

"*For the oppression of the poor, for the sighing of the needy, now will I arise, saith the Lord;* I will set him in safety from him that puffeth at him" (Psalms 12:5).

"*Trust not in oppression, and become not vain in robbery:* if riches increase, set not your heart upon them" (Psalms 62:10).

"*If thou seest the oppression of the poor,* and violent perverting of judgment and justice in a province, marvel not at the matter: for he that is higher than the highest regardeth; and there be higher than they" (Ecclesiastes 5:8).

"The people of the land have used oppression, and exercised robbery, *and have vexed the poor and needy: yea, they have oppressed the stranger wrongfully*" (Ezekiel 22:29).

"And seeing one of them suffer wrong, he defended him, and *avenged him that was oppressed,* and smote the Egyptian" (Acts 7:24).

"How God anointed Jesus of Nazareth with the Holy Ghost and with power: who went about doing good, and *healing all that were oppressed* of the devil; for God was with him" (Acts 10:38).

Riches

"*The blessing of the LORD, it maketh rich,* and he addeth no sorrow with it" (Proverbs 10:22).

"*There is that maketh himself rich,* yet hath nothing: there is that maketh himself poor, yet hath great riches" (Proverbs 13:7).

"The poor useth entreaties; *but the rich answereth roughly*" (Proverbs 18:23).

Riches continued

"He that loveth pleasure shall be a poor man: *he that loveth wine and oil shall not be rich*" (Proverbs 21:17).

"*Labor not to be rich*: cease from thine own wisdom" (Proverbs 23:4).

"Better is the poor that walketh in his uprightness, than he that is perverse in his ways, *though he be rich*" (Proverbs 28:6).

"*The rich man is wise in his own conceit;* but the poor that hath understanding searcheth him out" (Proverbs 28:11).

"A faithful man shall abound with blessings: *but he that maketh haste to be rich shall not be innocent*" (Proverbs 28:20).

"*He that hasteth to be rich hath an evil eye,* and considereth not that poverty shall come upon him" (Proverbs 28:22).

"Thus saith the Lord, Let not the wise man glory in his wisdom, neither let the mighty man glory in his might, *let not the rich man glory in his riches*" (Jeremiah 9:23).
"*For the rich men thereof are full of violence,* and the inhabitants thereof have spoken lies, and their tongue is deceitful in their mouth" (Micah 6:12).

"Whose possessors slay them, and hold themselves not guilty: and they that sell them say, *Blessed be the Lord; for I am rich: and their own shepherds pity them not*" (Zechariah 11:5).

"Then said Jesus unto his disciples, Verily I say unto you, *That a rich man shall hardly enter into the kingdom of heaven*" (Matthew 19:23).

"And when he heard this, *he was very sorrowful: for he was very rich*" (Luke 18:23)

"Hearken, my beloved brethren, *Hath not God chosen the poor of this world rich in faith*, and heirs of the kingdom which he hath promised to them that love him" (James 2:5)?

"But ye have despised the poor. Do *not rich men oppress you*, and draw you before the judgment seats" (James 2:6)?

"Go to now, *ye rich men, weep and howl for your miseries* that shall come upon you" (James 5:1).

"I know thy works, and tribulation, *and poverty, (but thou art rich)* and I know the blasphemy of them which say they are Jews, and are not, but are the synagogue of Satan" (Revelation 2:9)

"*Because thou sayest, I am rich, and increased with goods, and have need of nothing;* and knowest not that thou art wretched, and miserable, and poor, and blind, and naked" (Revelation 3:17)

"The merchants of these things, *which were made rich by her, shall stand afar off* for the fear of her torment, weeping and wailing" (Revelation 18:15)

"And the cares of this world, and *the deceitfulness of riches, and the lusts of other things entering in, choke the word,* and it becometh unfruitful" (Mark 4:19).

"*Now if the fall of them be the riches of the world,* and the diminishing of them the riches of the Gentiles; how much more their fullness" (Romans 11:12)?

"*Charge them that are rich in this world, that they be not highminded;* nor trust in uncertain riches, but in the living God, who giveth us richly all things to enjoy" (II Timothy 6:17).

SEEDTIME

Reward

"*Now this man purchased a field with the reward of iniquity*; and falling headlong, he burst asunder in the midst, and all his bowels gushed out" (Acts 1:18).

"Rejoice ye in that day, and leap for joy: for, behold, *your reward is great in heaven:* for in the like manner did their fathers unto the prophets" (Luke 6:23).

"*What is my reward then?* Verily that, when I preach the gospel, I may make the gospel of Christ without charge, that I abuse not my power in the gospel" (I Corinthians 9:18).

"And, behold, *I come quickly; and my reward is with me,* to give every man according as his work shall be" (Revelation 22:12).

"Therefore when thou doest thine alms, do not sound a trumpet before thee, as the hypocrites do in the synagogues and in the streets, that they may have glory of men. Verily I say unto you, *They have their reward*" (Matthew 6:2).

"But without faith it is impossible to please him : for he that cometh to God must believe that he is, and that *he is a rewarder of them that diligently seek him*" (Hebrews 11:6).

"Woe unto them! for they have gone in the way of Cain, *and ran greedily after the error of Balaam for reward, and perished in the gainsaying of Korah*" (Jude 1:11).

Spiritual Gifts

"For I long to see you, that I may impart unto you *some spiritual gift*, to the end ye may be established" (Romans 1:11).

"*Now concerning spiritual gifts,* brethren, I would not have you ignorant" (I Corinthians 12:1).

"*Follow after charity, and desire spiritual gifts,* but rather that ye may prophesy" (I Corinthians 14:1).

"Even so ye, *forasmuch as ye are zealous of spiritual gifts,* seek that ye may excel to the edifying of the church" (I Corinthians 14:12).

"Blessed be the God and Father of our Lord Jesus Christ, *who hath blessed us with all spiritual blessings* in heavenly places in Christ" (Ephesians 1:3).

"These all *died in faith, not having received the promises, but having seen them afar off,* and were persuaded of them, and embraced them, and confessed that they were strangers and pilgrims on the earth" (Hebrews 11:13).

"Whereby are given unto us *exceeding great and precious promises: that by these ye might be partakers of the divine nature,* having escaped the corruption that is in the world through lust" (II Peter 1:4).

"And Jesus answering said unto them, Render to Caesar the things that are Caesar's, *and to God the things that are God's.* And they marveled at him" (Mark 12:17).

Thought

"Therefore I say unto you, *Take no thought for your life,* what ye shall eat, or what ye shall drink; nor yet for your body, what ye shall put on. Is not the life more than meat, and the body than raiment" (Matthew 6:25)?

Thought continued

"Which of you by taking *thought* can add one cubit unto his stature" (Matthew 6:27)?

"*And why take ye thought for raiment?* Consider the lilies of the field, how they grow; they toil not, neither do they spin" (Matthew 6:28).

"*Therefore take no thought, saying, What shall we eat?* or, What shall we drink? or, Wherewithal shall we be clothed" (Matthew 6:31)?

"*Take therefore no thought for the morrow:* for the morrow shall take thought for the things of itself. Sufficient unto the day is the evil thereof" (Matthew 6:34).

"Forasmuch then as we are the offspring of God, *we ought not to think that the Godhead is like unto gold, or silver, or stone, graven by art and man's device*" (Acts 17:29).

"*If any man think himself to be a prophet, or spiritual,* let him acknowledge that the things that I write unto you are the commandments of the Lord" (I Corinthians 14:37).

"*For if a man think himself to be something, when he is nothing,* he deceiveth himself" (Galatians 6:3).

"Now unto him that is able to do exceeding abundantly *above all that we ask or think,* according to the power that worketh in us" (Ephesians 3:20).

"*Do ye think that the Scripture saith in vain,* The spirit that dwelleth in us lusteth to envy" (James 4:5)?

"Wherein *they think it strange that ye run not with them to the same excess of riot,* speaking evil of you" (I Peter 4:4).

"Finally, brethren, whatsoever things are true, whatsoever things are honest, whatsoever things are just, whatsoever things are pure, whatsoever things are lovely, whatsoever things are of good report; if there be any virtue, and if there be any praise, *think on these things"* (Philippians 4:8).

Treasures

"Then Jesus beholding him loved him, and said unto him, One thing thou lackest: go thy way, sell whatsoever thou hast, and give to the poor, *and thou shalt have treasure in heaven:* and come, take up the cross, and follow me" (Mark 10:21).

"Treasures of wickedness profit nothing: but righteousness delivereth from death" (Proverbs 10:2).

"Ye shall not make with me *gods of silver, neither shall ye make unto you gods of gold"* (Exodus 20:23).

"And Moses returned unto the LORD, and said, Oh, this people have sinned a great sin, and *have made them gods of gold"* (Exodus 32:31).

"Lay not up for yourselves treasures upon earth, where moth and rust doth corrupt, and where thieves break through and steal" (Matthew 6:19).

"But lay up for yourselves treasures in heaven, where neither moth nor rust doth corrupt, and where thieves do not break through nor steal" (Matthew 6:20).

"In whom are hid all the *treasures of wisdom and knowledge"* (Colossians 2:3).

SEEDTIME

Treasures continued

"Esteeming the reproach of *Christ greater riches than the treasures in Egypt*: for he had respect unto the recompense of the reward" (Hebrews 11:26).

Vanity

"*Wealth gotten by vanity shall be diminished*: but he that gathereth by labor shall increase" (Proverbs 13:11).

"*The getting of treasures by a lying tongue is a vanity* tossed to and fro of them that seek death" (Proverbs 21:6).

"*Remove far from me vanity and lies*: give me neither poverty nor riches; feed me with food convenient for me" (Proverbs 30:8).

"Therefore I hated life; because the work that is wrought under the sun is grievous unto me: *for all is vanity and vexation of spirit*" (Ecclesiastes 2:17).

"He that loveth silver shall not be satisfied with silver; nor he that loveth abundance with increase: *this is also vanity*" (Ecclesiastes 5:10).

"Better is the sight of the eyes than the wandering of the desire: *this is also vanity and vexation of spirit*" (Ecclesiastes 6:9).

"They that make a graven image are *all of them vanity; and their delectable things shall not profit;* and they are their own witnesses; they see not, nor know; that they may be ashamed" (Isaiah 44:9).

"*They are vanity, the work of errors:* in the time of their visitation they shall perish" (Jeremiah 51:18).

"Therefore thus saith the Lord GOD; *Because ye have spoken vanity, and seen lies, therefore, behold, I am against you,* saith the Lord God" (Ezekiel 13:8).

"*For the idols have spoken vanity,* and the diviners have seen a lie, and have told false dreams; they comfort in vain: therefore they went their way as a flock, they were troubled, because there was no shepherd" (Zechariah 10:2).

"For the creature was *made subject to vanity, not willingly, but by reason of him who hath subjected the same in hope*" (Romans 8:20).

"This I say therefore, and testify in the Lord, that ye henceforth walk not as other Gentiles walk, in *the vanity of their mind*" (Ephesians 4:17).

"*For when they speak great swelling words of vanity, they allure through the lusts of the flesh, through much wantonness,* those that were clean escaped from them who live in error" (II Peter 2:18).

Wealth

"And God said to Solomon, Because this was in thine heart, *and thou hast not asked riches, wealth, or honor,* nor the life of thine enemies, neither yet hast asked long life; but hast asked wisdom and knowledge for thyself, that thou mayest judge my people, over whom I have made thee king" (II Chronicles 1:11).

"*Let no man seek his own, but every man another's wealth*" (I Corinthians 10:24).

SEEDTIME

Wealth continued

"Now therefore give not your daughters unto their sons, neither take their daughters unto your sons, *nor seek their peace or their wealth forever: that ye may be strong,* and eat the good of the land, and leave it for an inheritance to your children forever" (Ezra 9:12).

"*They that trust in their wealth,* and boast themselves in the multitude of their riches; None of them can by any means redeem his brother, nor give to God a ransom for him" (Psalms 49:6-7).

"*A man to whom God hath given riches, wealth, and honor, so that he wanteth nothing for his soul* of all that he desireth, yet God giveth him not power to eat thereof, but a stranger eateth it: this is vanity, and it is an evil disease" (Ecclesiastes 6:2).

SEEDTIME
Isaiah 46:5-11

"To whom will ye liken me, and make me equal, and compare me, that we may be like? They lavish gold out of the bag, and weigh silver in the balance, and hire a goldsmith; and he makes it a god: they fall down, yea, they worship. They bear him upon the shoulder, they carry him, and set him in his place, and he stand; from his place shall he not remove: yea, one shall cry unto him, yet can he not answer, nor save him out of his trouble. Remember this, and show yourselves men: bring it again to mind, O ye transgressors. Remember the former things of old: for I am God, and there is none else; I am God, and there is none like me, Declaring the end from the beginning, and from ancient times the things that are not yet done, saying, My counsel shall stand, and I will do all my pleasure: Calling a ravenous bird from the east, the man that executes my counsel from a far country: yea, I have spoken it , I will also bring it to pass; I have purposed it , I will also do it."